I Dare To Heal

With Compassionate Love

Joel Vorensky

Life's Breath Publications
San Diego, California

I Dare To Heal.

First Edition.

The information in this publication is not a substitute for professional medical or psychological advice or service. A physician or professional therapist should be consulted before attempting any of the suggestions or techniques discussed in this book. The author and publisher disclaim any liability arising directly or indirectly from the use of this book.

Published by:
Life's Breath Publications
6394 Rancho Mission Rd. Suite #116
San Diego, CA 92108

Subtitled "With Compassionate Love"
ISBN: 0-9704510-9-1

Additional copies of this book may be ordered directly from the publisher for $14.95 each, by calling: 1-866-292-8022. <info@IDareToHeal.com>.

Publisher's Cataloging-in-Publication
(Provided by Quality Books, Inc.)

Vorensky, Joel.
    "I dare to heal" : with compassionate love / by Joel
Vorensky. — 1st ed.
    p. Cm.
    Includes bibliographical references and index.
    ISBN 0-9704510-9-1

    1. Vorensky, Joel. 2. Self-actualization
(Psychology) 3. Healers—United States—Biography.
4. Teachers—United States—Biography. 5. Counselors—
United States—Biography. 6. Spiritual life.
I. Title

BF1408.2V67A3 2001   291.4'092
                                             QBI00-901748

Printed in the United States of America

Testimonials

I've been a leader in the personal growth Rebirthing movement for a period of 23 years. Rebirthing is the most powerful emotional healing process I've ever been exposed to. Rebirthing is a powerful and dynamic process that results in profound healing and spiritual growth. Mr. Vorensky's book I Dare to Heal *describes the benefits of this ancient breath process. I recommend the reading of Mr. Vorensky's book.*

— Cass Smith, Sadhana Fellowship

Joel is a sensitive caring man committed to his personal and spiritual growth. His book inspires and encourages us all as we journey together.

— Angela Geary, Transformational Counselor

As a breathing and emotions therapist, I have seen Joel confront his issues with a commitment and a passion that have been admirable! He is, indeed, a courageous man.

— Barbara Fox White, M.A.

Having been a practitioner of T'ai Chi Chih and Qigong for twenty years, I have experienced many wonderful changes in my life and my attitude. I have found that these practices reduce stress and bring calmness to my life that allows me to experience more happiness and inner peace. Joel Vorensky speaks of the benefits of T'ai Chi Chih and other breathing methods in this book, I Dare to Heal. *I know he too has personally experienced the loving power of T'ai Chi Chih. I know he too has personally experienced the joy and calmness produced by these practices. I encourage you to read his book, which offers many ideas that you too can add to your life so you too can live a life of true happiness and peace.*

— Susan Patterson, Teacher of T'ai Chi Chih / Qigong

What a treasure it is to find contained in this single source such a comprehensive gathering of practical and effective tools to assist and empower our spiritual perfection. Great encouragement, and an inspiration to 'GO FOR IT' can be found in the enjoyment of this book.

— Syhd Clopton, Miracles Retreats Leader,
Course in Miracles Facilitator

Joel's sense of being, his oneness to the flowing tides of conscious existence and spiritual enlightenment, reclaims the vitality of our essence and provides purpose to those lives lacking identity.

— Christopher Rogers, CSR Productions

The Hebrew word for mending, healing, and transformation is Tikkun. In Jewish mystical practice, the purpose of life is to heal our soul, and to heal the world. Joel Vorensky has written I Dare to Heal *for just that purpose. Joel is a wonderful storyteller, teacher and ecstatic being. In this autobiography we can experience how he has mended, healed, and transformed his life. His story teaches us to turn problems into opportunities. Then, as the psalms say, we can truly 'treasure each day', holding our dark side with understanding and compassion, and opening ourselves to the wisdom and love of the light.*

— Burton Bialik, Ph.D., MFCC., Certified Group Psychotherapist

I Dare to Heal *is a deeply revealing and compelling invitation to the profound healing power of Breath Work and Rebirthing. With sensitivity, vulnerability, and genuine love, author Joel Vorensky accurately describes the incredible transformational journey that is available and that has been so beneficial to many thousands.*

I highly recommend this beautiful book to anyone who is sincerely seeking to free themselves from emotional pain from the past or the present. You will be inspired.

— Robert Frey, MA, Ph.D. Candidate
International Tantra Teacher, Author, and Counselor

I recommend the reading of I Dare to Heal. *I have seen how Mr. Vorensky has benefitted in his physical, emotional, and spiritual development from his participation in Tae Kwon-Do. I believe you too can benefit from the practice of this martial art.*

— Mustapha Abdulíjalil
Master Instructor, Tae Kwon-Do

I Dare To Heal is a remarkable book. I am familiar with most of the techniques it mentions, but I have never before seen all of them discussed in the same place. The author's description of his own experience with them gives a valuable insight into what expeiences others can expect. Joel Vorensky has written a very useful book.

— Robert Goodman
President, San Diego Publishers Alliance

My mission is to empower others to make the most of their lives by sharing my loving insight. To that end I dedicate this story to all who are truly searching for self-realization, to all committed to serious in-depth self-exploration, and also to all who simply desire to live fully, relax and enjoy life. It is my hope that what I've learned about myself may help others have faith and experience true self-discovery. It is my prayer! It is the motivation behind every word written on the pages of this book. In deference to others, in this story I have amended names, circumstances and situations to protect individual sensitivities. I have come to love my fellow travelers dearly.

We are embarking together on an inspirational spiritual journey. I do not claim to be a guru or a saint, but a teacher, writer, and counselor. Enjoy the journey!

Contents

Foreword

Joel Vorensky explores the sacred work of embodying Spirit, marrying body and soul to experience the fullest, richest potential of life. He illuminates the realms of spirituality, pleasure, and desire with the sites of our greatest fears, yearnings, satisfactions, and misunderstandings. Honoring both the linear analytical mind and the creatively chaotic mind, he shows how we must recognize and unite our passionate 'dark' and serene 'light' aspects to become whole and healthy spiritual beings.

I Dare to Heal, is an inspirational guide to wholeness. Joel invites us to become spacious enough to embody the entire drama of our personal and collective soul. *I Dare to Heal* is a magnetic field of wisdom and vision.

—Kennedy Carr
Personal Growth Trainer/Counselor

A Prelude to Our Journey Together

Hello, kindred spirit. My name is Joel.

I am a Time Traveler. My journey began long ago—and not so long ago. Although I feel as if I've lived an eternity, I am young in spirit. Like you, I am ancient in time and space. Born on the cusp of Scorpio and Sagittarius, it is my nature to live a life filled with passion, sensitivity and emotion.

I believe in a higher power that speaks to me. I listen. That, in short, is how this story came to be.

I believe in love. I know how to give and receive warm, tender, caring and attentive affection naturally. Love has made me vulnerable and given me a sense of owning my own authority. My vulnerability enables me to express my deepest thoughts and feelings toward others.

This story flows from my love and vulnerability.

Though I am a spiritual being, I am practical and well anchored in my own sense of existence, and I have found a deep and abiding sense of peace within myself. Being spiritual does not mean being weird or ungrounded in reality. Indeed, I have found that reality and spirituality are congruent with each other, hence I am practical in the ways of the world. My personal peace and bliss flow from knowing I am intimately connected to the universal source of life itself—the Ultimate Reality. I have been created by that ultimate source of life to love myself, others, and especially things of the spirit.

It behooves me to stay intimately in touch with these most precious of human qualities, as they bring wholeness to all I do. Walking in this sense of wholeness enables me each day to work more successfully through my pain.

> *There is strong shadow*
> *Where there is much light!*

> —Johann Wolfgang Von Goethe

I count the following methodologies and technologies among those that have been invaluable in helping me achieve my humanistic goals: emotional release techniques such as Rebirthing, Healing Breath Work, Primal Therapy; meditation; Tae Kwon Do and T'ai Chi Chih; acupuncture; Dances of Universal Peace ('Sufi dancing'); Peer Co-Counseling and relationship counseling; devotional singing; Sacred Ceremonial Sweat Lodge; A Course in Miracles; Reiki; Reflexology; laughter; drumming; and Iyengar and Vini Yoga.

These and other processes have helped me in mastering life's issues, healing naturally and controlling aging. They have helped me to take control of my mind! I believe the integration of these methods in your life can help you to free more of yourself from daily stresses and past distresses so you can begin to love yourself more powerfully.

As you learn to connect appropriately with your feelings and release them, you are sure to experience heightened personal growth, self-realization, enlightenment and spiritual connection with a Higher Power.

I enjoy letting go of my feelings. It is my freedom. It liberates me from any internal sense of invalidation and opens me up to growing in genuine self-love. My feelings flow from layers of distress, cascading from within me like a purifying waterfall, ever emanating from the deepest layers of my unconscious. Releasing these feelings strengthens me by enabling me to truly connect with Spirit in my daily meditations. I achieve wholeness through this act of freeing self, *Daring to Heal*, and loving powerfully!

I am inspired when I listen to those who speak intelligently and act from their hearts. Responding with conviction and fully loving intelligence toward those who speak dogmatically from their intellect has not always been so easy for me. Learning to do so has been an arduous journey, but one I have come to love.

A talent is formed in stillness,
A character in the world's torrent.

—Johann Wolfgang Von Goethe

It is said that the greatest personal growth takes place under the most difficult and challenging of circumstances. I have found this to be true in every sense. I am a particularly sensitive man, and countless challenging experiences have brought me turmoil. Thanks to my tenacious commitment to life, I have come to see obstacles as opportunities for growth, and in the face of adversity and sorrow I have grown immensely.

But he/she that dare not grasp the thorn
Should never crave the rose.

—-Anne Bronte

Human feelings come in an endless variety of depths, degrees, and dimensions. They are the energies of creation we all share. We are one great family; hence, whatever is helpful to one in shaping these energies to create a more rewarding life can be helpful to others as well.

As human beings we have choice: we can harbor our feelings, or release them. We can choose to invest them in healthy or unhealthy ways. Life is nothing if not an ongoing series of experiences, energies and choices. (There is no 'good' or 'bad' in this—'good' and 'bad' are human judgments, and as such they have nothing to do with actual reality.)

My barriers have been blown away. There is no limit now to what I dare to feel, or to the degree, depth, or dimension of trauma I am willing to explore. My dynamic transformation has taken me into more realized states of consciousness.

This is my birthright, and with tenacity I continue to explore yet uncharted unconscious states of mind. The exploration of inner space is perhaps the most dramatic and fulfilling adventure known to human kind. I have embarked on this adventure of self-discovery as life beckons me forward to a vast variety of new choices. The only limit seems to be my own ability to intelligently consider new alternatives.

Although some of your life challenges may not be fun, your distresses and traumas are inevitably the very precursors of meaningful development. Through the cleansing of the self through the release of pain you can come to experience joy, bliss and a greater empowerment of love.

This is but one of many routes to discovering greater love. Another way would be to transcend your issues. My favorite way of uncovering the empowerment of love is through willful expression of love to oneself, others, and Spirit.

The history of the world is none other than the progress of the Consciousness of Freedom.

—Georg Wilhelm Friedrich Hegel

This book is the story of my journey that I began in 1968. It is also a journey from spirit to spirit, from me to you, and beyond to all those around us who have a want, a desire, a need for freedom from inhibiting, inflexible, self-defeating thought patterns. It is designed to build and release your courage—the courage to feel what needs to be felt to allow you to experience freedom; the courage to act on your intentions in the world; the courage to take reasonable risks and make the choices necessary to truly *live* life. Integrating personal growth methodologies into your life-style will help you find the courage to speak with conviction, without doubt or reservation, in loving tones, without allowing fear to suppress your spontaneous impulses. It will also give you the courage and emotional strength to endure-even appreciate-humiliation and failure.

As I reach out to you, I think of my dear friend 'Steven,' who is often uptight and on edge, so anxious about himself and others that he cannot enjoy life. I also think of Mark, so insecure he cannot find happiness or peace, who speaks often of the great needs in his life that others have not met. I think of 'Laura,' who, in spite of great distress has consistently stayed connected to Spirit and maintained a loving and endearing connection to the world. Do my friends sound familiar to you? They should. Their problems are the same as those facing every man, woman and child.

I've met many who seem to be 'on hold' in their lives. Like untimely callers, they await an answer that doesn't come. Constrained from within, they shrink from feeling what needs to be felt to gain true freedom. The possibility of freedom can be scary to the uninitiated. There are those who suffer from 'mood disorders.' Many are just plain 'stuck' and unable (for a plethora of reasons) to help themselves. They may desire freedom and have an intellectual understanding that the only way to achieve it is to face their inner conflicts, yet they procrastinate on their intentions to act on their own behalf. In the absence of tools and resources to help them, who can blame them?

They need a 'helper.' Let it be me. Or you.

To those who are critical and afraid of attaining personal growth through metaphysical or personal growth techniques, I say this: there is nothing to fear. I pray you will listen to your heart and not follow your mind's fearful, negative and critical-thoughts, thoughts rooted in doubt and despair.

My journey of learning how to love myself took time, and yours will as well. In the process I have come to see myself as a Time Traveler, a ruthless, unyielding seeker of self. I have claimed the right of passage for my journey. I send you my blessings for yours.

There is a Sanskrit saying "Let all the beings in all the worlds be happy and let all the beings in all the worlds have peace". I would like to add have faith as well.

Acknowledgments

I would like to acknowledge all of those who have made my journeys through time and across the face of this earth meaningful, truthful and joyous.

In particular, I acknowledge the following:

Mom, for making room for me;
Dad, for living a life of determination, patience and courage;
Lina, my daughter, whom I love dearly;
Spirit, for infusing me with joy and blissful hope;
All of my loving friends;
Men and women in the caring professions;
Harvey Jackins, founder of Re-Evaluation Co-Counseling;
Lou Solis, Director, The Life Institute, Oceanside, CA;

Charles McReynolds, my dear friend and Peer Co-Counselor;
The Reader, for joining me on this, our first journey together.

Joel Vorensky
San Diego, California,
January 2001

one

The Trauma of Being Born

Before you can reach to the top of a tree and understand the
buds and flowers, you will have to go deep to the roots, because
the secret lies there. And the deeper the roots, the higher the tree.

—Nietzsche

"I'm sorry, my dear. Your womb is so very small. Inordinately small. I'm afraid you will never carry a child to full term."

His words rang in her ears like a death sentence. "Inordinately small... never carry a child...."

She sought opinions from other doctors, hoping for another verdict. Their words were different, but they always carried the same meaning. One physician told her she had an 'infantile womb'.

She didn't care about the size of her womb! All she wanted was to bear a child, to fulfill her destiny as a woman, and to bring her husband an heir to the family name. She made up her mind to prove the doctors wrong. She would have a child!

Ultimately she succeeded in realizing her dream. I am the child she wanted so badly. This is my story.

Thanks to years of intense work on my inner self and the skillful guidance of a number of facilitators, I have succeeded at last in connecting with and releasing the trauma I suffered during conception, gestation and birth. I am now intuitively connected to and in touch with all of the various aspects of the experience.

As if it weren't enough that I should have to make my entrance into this world through my mother's 'infantile womb', my trauma

was accentuated by her post-partum psychosis. Her troubles were undoubtedly caused by her attending physician's use of a drug combination of morphine and scopolamine called "Twilight Sleep" that gives
rise to depression, amnesia and hallucinations.

As I muse on the miracle of having come through it, I feel a celebration within me. In my mind I am waltzing with a pretty, young
woman. The universe opens, and Spirit takes charge as we circle the
dance floor. Space is timeless, ever expanding. Our eyes meet with
fixed gaze, knowing intuitively that there is a spiritual significance
to the moment. Words depart.

This waltz connects me to the celebration that took place during
my conception!

Whenever life gets really tough for me, I find it nurturing to reconnect intuitively with my dawning experiences. It is an exercise in tra-
versing the boundaries of time and space—a leap forward to hope
and vision, a leap backward through experiential time, and a leap
within to unite future, present and past.

I have found recalling my bold entrance into life to be powerful for
maintaining my faith, hope and vision while offering strength during times of insecurity.

I am not the first to consider and apply the force of birth, in the dimension of time past, to bring its power to bear upon the present. David, in the book of Psalms, said:

> *I praise you because I am fearfully and wonderfully made; your
> works are wonderful, I know that full well.*
> *My frame was not hidden from you when I was made in the secret
> place. When I was woven together in the depths of the earth, your
> eyes saw my unformed body.*
> *All the days ordained for me were written in your book before one of
> them came to be.*

The primary methodology I use to draw upon the creative force of
my natal experience is known as *Rebirthing*, or **Healing Breath.**
This method involves the physiological process of inhaling and exhaling in a circular pattern, creating a channel for emotional time
travel through layers of distress awaiting discovery and release.

My first Rebirthing experience returned me to nine months of terror:

Confined in total darkness, infant Joel suffocates. There is no room for him to grow and develop. He must struggle to exist simply.

I feel like screaming out from the darkness. My thought is, "I was fine as I was, just let me grow! I was fine as I was, Mamma! Stop pressing!" The walls of the womb press in ever more firmly on my infant self as I develop in size. Will I survive?

By connecting my inhalations and exhalations I relive the experience in moments. I continue my circular breathing. Again and again, suffocating, my infant mind and body struggle against their confinement.

Anger. Rage. I need space! I feel the tenacious primal life force taking charge as my will to live manifests.

Is there no limit to the emotions crashing like waves within me? My feet begin to kick. Deep penetrating sounds emanate from infant Joel's stomach chest and abdominal cavity filling my adult ears. Fear and anger disseminate.

I journey through the birth canal. Once again, there is darkness and limited air supply. The walls press in around me. "I can't move!"

Again, terror grips my infant mind. " Am I dying?" I don't know. Fluid fills my mouth and throat. Terrified, I choke in fear. My body is distorted beyond my control as my mother's intense contractions inch me ahead.

Onward I am pushed, gasping for a breath of life I panic. The air allowing me to survive this traumatic event might be coming from the placenta. Its supply cannot holdout forever.

I continue the circular breathing. Moving onward through the birth canal, I wonder. "Will there be light at the end of this tunnel? Will there be an end to this struggle?"

I inhale strongly. Upon exhaling, a terrifying sound wells from within me. I take a 'power breath', nine quick, forceful inhales and exhales followed by a final inhale. At the end, I hold my breath and tighten my muscles-until an attending facilitator signals for the final release. I can feel my terror evaporating as I connect with a more profound emotional outlet.

My ears are assaulted by screams that shake me to my core. My mother's pained screams. "Will they never end?" I feel them take root within my psyche.

"Help me! Get me out! It is too much to bear!"

Her screams pierce in rapid succession, penetrating my remembrance. Inhaling brings me to a state at which the horror of her screams and my fears of suffocation and confinement simultaneously descend upon me. My own shrieks reverberate through the room. Now, I scream into a pillow, so no one is disturbed around me.

These feelings are painful, and deep-rooted, yet I proceed. I move into this traumatic black hole time and again with my breath work.

I emerge to see my mother's face staring at me an image of terror. Contorted, her face forever leaves its footprint upon my psyche, giving rise to this deafening sound. Our scream! My scream!

The image multiplies in my mind. I inhale to connect with it. The child inside, emotionally devastated child sees these images and cries out.

"There is no pain! No pain"

The breath has brought me through the terror, cleared the subconscious, freed the spirit and strengthened in soul. I sit up. Looking out the window I see McDonald's and a sign reading: 'Protege Tu Futuro, USE Condones', a message about protecting life through the use of common sense and contraception. Four palm trees stand under the billboard, branches motionless on a quiet Sunday night. Two couples converse at a table in the cool evening air.

In, Out, In, Out.

Teresa, my facilitator, encourages me to continue the circular breathing. I inhale and exhale forcefully nine times, then hold the tenth.

This 'power breath' brings me face to face with the terrifying image of my mother's contorted face. My body rocks. My feet kick as I release the terror from the depths of my power center.

I cleanse my mind with my screams, peeling away layer upon layer of trauma, and relaxing as the distress simply falls away like the skin of an onion. The core of my disturbance is revealed.

I have felt an electrical charge and sensations of empowerment running through my body during this breath session. I have received a gift from the universe. It feels remarkable. I have experienced my birth as bliss, a dance, a celebration.

Once again, I have drawn my first breath of life. Life flows in on a beautiful, crisp, clear, cool and sunlit morning after a deeply refreshing night of rest! This joyous breaking forth is available to us all. We must simply choose to breathe the breath of real life once again.

What an uplifting, eternally joyous experience it has been to be conceived and born!

I have since experienced many such 'rebirths' through which I have released enormous amounts of self-pity and pent-up destructive emotions. My birth trauma left me feeling isolated, and with a chronic necessity for warmth, love, and nurturing—nurturing I have learned to give myself following many years of hard work! In terms of physical health, my asthma, engendered by my highly restrained and restricted birthing experience, has been relegated to the status of 'just a memory'.

I have become free and whole.

Healing Practice: Rebirthing and Healing Breath Work

Much of my own emotional release and profound personal growth has been accomplished through Rebirthing and Healing Breath Work. These two modalities are similar in that both make use of a continuous inhale and exhale breathing pattern. In Rebirthing the person is encouraged to release feelings through sound, while in Healing Breath Work there may not be a release through sound; instead the person cuts through the emotions to the spirit and soul and the experience of profound self-love. Using both methods, I find them effective.

Rebirthing is a several thousand-year-old process brought to North America by Dr. Leonard Orr. Dr. Stanislav Grof, formerly Chief of Psychiatric Research at the Maryland Psychiatric Research Center and Assistant Professor of Psychiatry at Johns Hopkins University School of Medicine, wrote several books addressing the scope of this process over a period of thirty years. Dr. Grof speaks to the themes of freeing self and time travel in his book, *The Adventure of Self-Discovery*.

On a physiological level, breath is vital to life. When we inhale, we bring in life-supporting oxygen; when we exhale, we purge our bodies of carbon dioxide, nitrogen and other toxic gases and contaminates. There is much more to breathing than that, however. The conscious use of breath can put us in touch with the universal aspects of Spirit by allowing us to access, connect with and release feelings associated with the distress that lies within the multitude of realms of our consciousness. (It is interesting to note that in many languages the word for 'breath' is the same as the word for 'spirit'.)

The breathing process used in Rebirthing is deliberately continuous and circular. Inhaling has the effect of opening the self to feelings requiring release, and exhaling accomplishes the release. On the inhale, the participant completely fills their belly and chest cavity with God's given breath; exhaling, they surrender with a sigh, releasing any sounds that come through. The ongoing circular breath creates a vacuum or envelope within which the participant can relax into their feelings and achieve a natural release and cleansing of distress. Initially, rapid breaths may be used to circumvent defense and control mechanisms that can otherwise prevent access to one's feelings. Once relaxation and release have been accomplished, a variety of breathing rhythms may be introduced. Each person finds their own natural breathing rhythm, one that facilitates the release of emotions. Practice brings confidence and trust in a variety of rhythms, each having its own purpose. In essence there are the qualities of *intention, surrender, the passion of compassion, faith, self-discipline* and *tenacity* to make the process effective.

Breath Work requires maintenance of a conscious enthusiastic intent to release old emotions. The body may experience uncontrollable twitching and other forms of movement. Regardless of the body's manifestations, breath needs to be continuous. Practicing bio-energetic exercises (see below) before and during breath sessions as needed can aid significantly in releasing stored emotion.

Rebirthing, Breath Work is especially effective for those individuals experiencing Post-Traumatic Stress Disorder, or PTSD. PTSD afflicts those who served in combat or those who have been assaulted. There are a number of symptoms. These include re-experiencing traumatic events by mental images, heighten anxiety, nightmares, and avoiding the physical sites of where the trauma occurred. Breath Work accesses the anxiety and can powerfully release its energy. The transforming power of the process can speed up and relieve the profound affliction of PTSD.

Rebirthing, Breath Work is also effective in resolving depression. I have experienced depression as a child and as an adult because of on-going life situations of helplessness or powerlessness, for example, underemployment or unemployment. I've suppressed fear, grief, and anger. When I've released my feelings by way of the rebirthing, healing breath work, liberation from depression has always resulted. Nurturing spiritual faith, realizing limitations, having patience, being persistent and persevering can preclude unhealthy feelings that lead to depression.

Rebirthing is often done as a group process conducted by skilled, loving facilitators in a partially light filled room with relaxing music playing in the background. All participants agree to honor the confidentiality of the session. Facilitators honor each participant's humanness and give total respect to the capacity of the individual to access and release their emotions. An individual who has learned the process may choose to act as his or her own facilitator in a private session.

Rebirthing can produce profound results when used in conjunction with Positive Affirmations, Primal Scream, Peer Co-Counseling and/or a mirror-processes I will discuss later in this book. The combination of these modalities has led to my cleansing of chronic and intermittent distresses and to my sense of connecting with TIMELESS ENDLESS NOTHINGNESS IN MY INTERNAL CONSCIOUSNESS. I have found this to be the essence of an enlightened state of being.

I personally participate in a seventeen-year-old fellowship of Rebirthers known as Sadhana Fellowship. ('Sadhana' is the Sanskrit word for spiritual process). In subsequent chapters I will be sharing with you more of my own Rebirthing experiences, as well as those of other people whose lives I have touched.

Healing Practice: Bioenergetic Exercises

Breath work sessions can challenge the ego, and can challenge any inner emotional resistance (defense or control mechanisms) to access your stressful or distressful feelings. While the ego and the resistance to accessing your feelings may serve you well in many ways i.e., keeping you safe in the realm of the 'tried and true'. It also can hold you back when you want to make change. One must find ways to throw it off guard. One tool for achieving this is a set of bioenergetic exercises that can be used proceeding a breath work session and at any time during the session when the ego (the thoughts) refuses to continue the circular breath.

Bioenergetic exercises include:

• Standing, Arms extended (or fists placed in the lower back)-inhale as you bend your knees and exhale as you rise to a standing position.

- Pelvic Thrust: Standing, hands at waist, exhale as you thrust pelvis forward, inhale as you come back into your original position.
- Standing: Inhale and exhale as you lean your back against the wall with your chest open, knees bent.
- Rag Doll: Bend from the waist like a rag doll with your knees together and toes together, exhale as you bend down and inhaling as you straighten up.
- Cat: On your hands and knees, inhale as you lower your head and arch your back up and then exhale as you relax your back and raise your face to the sky. The goal is to free emotional blockage in the chakras to connect with the abdominal power center.

Points To Ponder

We can learn much about ourselves and speed up our personal development by exploring emotions relating to our conception, fetal development and birth. Consider the following questions:

- Is it possible that your present self-defeating behavior can stem from your conception, prenatal and birth experiences?
- Could your mother's use of drugs (prescribed or otherwise) have impacted you —or her, physically and emotionally?
- Could your development from conception through your formative years have impacted you in negative ways even now?

The answers to these questions may not be available to you in your present state of awareness. My own answers (as well as the questions themselves) arose out of intensive Rebirthing sessions I began as an adult. I highly recommend this work to you as a way of discovering and mitigating the impact of birth and early childhood trauma on your present life.

Two

Separation Before Unity

Pluck from the memory a rooted sorrow,
Canst thou not minister to a mind diseased?
Raze out the written troubles of the brain,
And with some sweet oblivious antidote
Cleanse the stuffed blossom of that perilous stuff
Which weighs upon the heart?

— William Shakespeare

The umbilical cord is cut.

I know the trauma of separation. I feel the loneliness of the world, and give out an instinctive and emotionally shattering scream.

It is so cold, so very, very cold.

As an adult I have always found it difficult to live in a cold climate—the cold weather triggers the terror of the cold I felt at birth. This is undoubtedly one reason I make my present residence in a warm climate.

My infant screams echo again and again as I release my terror of separating from the warm, nurturing womb. I enjoy an immediate cleansing, a momentary release that will have to hold me until I can complete the freeing of my soul from this trauma by means of the circular breath.

A tiny sparrow chirps happily inside the nest outside the window. It is springtime and the sparrow family has found a nest abandoned by previous residents, hidden from other birds of prey, high above the patio overlooking Mission Valley in beautiful San Diego, California. An aromatic grove of wispy gray-green eucalyptus trees sends its scent on the soft gusts of wind flowing through the canyon.

The sparrow seems content, its watchful gaze penetrating its surroundings in search of potential dangers. The nest must be kept safe for the babies, who need the nurturing and warmth of the mother.

Father Sparrow is most likely out seeking food for the babies. He is always watchful and ready to protect his newborns from danger.

Against this backdrop I travel through time to see myself lying alone in my crib. I am depressed. There is no mother near. My mother is away in the hospital, suffering post-partum depression

I begin my circular breathing once again, deliberately moving into the depression of separation from my mother. The thought comes again and again: "Where are you, Mamma?"

Pangs of grief and fear rise from within as I express my sadness.

Fear, grief, rage! The paranoia comes and goes. It comes with the pauses between my breaths, and again during rest periods between breath sessions.

I exhale to release the paranoia. The trauma within me sheds another layer of shell. Another level of healing is achieved.

I am so tired. Emotional release is exhausting. It's time to rest. True rest is essential for meaningful living. Solomon, the wise man and renowned teacher and philosopher said, *"There is a time for every purpose under heaven!"* There is a time to work and a time to rest!

I watch the birds communicating with each other on the balcony. One chirps pitifully in its need.

I too am in need.

I begin again to breathe with a deep inhale and exhale life's toxins, pains and pressures to the universe. Like that bird, I express my need. The pain is released with each round of harsh cries emanating from the depths of my inner self. My need sounds ever more intense, ever deeper and more powerful within me: *"I need, I need, Mamma, Mamma, I need, I need!"*

This is not a hollow cry. Something is happening inside of me!

I feel my life's very source of power being restored to me upon each releasing breath. I feel an infinite spiritual connection forming, a bridge being reinforced, reaching out and transcending time and space. I am being touched by a spiritual presence, one I can only call Infinite Love. I feel a flowing of the love of life itself, a love that embodies the essence of creation.

Such a release of emotional energy gives way to an immeasurable peace within. Finally! Tranquillity, peacefulness, and a resting-place to dwell in.

Touching Spirit surpasses any sexual or physical experience known to the human creature. It is the ultimate 'resting in release'.

I have become the infant Joel. I am Joel, but fully restored!

There is no longer any separation.

There is only oneness.

I am connected.

I am here for myself now.

I've earned my right of passage. I have achieved the vital connection between my inner infant, child and the infinite Spirit of life. I am now my own loving mother, connected to and nurturing my inner child!

Points To Ponder

Physical separation from your mother at the time of the cutting of the umbilical cord can create emotional trauma. Ask yourself:

- What effect could your separation from your mother's body at birth have had on you as an emotional being?
- How has this separation affected your behavior?

Three

Time Travel

There is a way of breathing that's a shame and suffocation.
And there's another way of expiring, A Love Breath,
That lets you open infinitely.

Rumi

Back, back, back, traveling through time. Where will my circular breathing take me this time?

Not all circular breathing sessions take you back to release trauma. Today I may encounter acute and expressive sensations of joy and bliss. Sensations of celebration, zest, enthusiasm, and the flow of life energies often follow on the heels of release of trauma.

I travel in time through a relaxed inhale and express my emotions with passion upon the sigh and surrender of the ensuing exhale. The ongoing circular breathing enables my time travel and creates the connections with my emotions. The breath becomes a channel, a vacuum, and a wormhole to the primal life force itself, what the Chinese call *'chi'*.

My time travels are never dull. They are always exciting, challenging, new, cleansing. They always promote the re-emergence of a part of myself that has been obscured by distress. Time Traveling can be mystical. At times the colors span the entire range of the rainbow. The 'pot of gold' at the end is the feeling of being uplifted and connected to Spirit.

I am no saint. I am but a man who consistently chooses life, in all its expressions, and refuses to merely survive from day to day. My life is so much more than today or tomorrow, for I am a time traveler. I breathe in time and eternity with all the feelings they possess, and the emotion released propels me forward in a powerful expression of all the feelings I have embraced.

Breath Work is the gateway to a vision of Spirit without boundaries. It is the breath of life! Cleansing trauma is the gateway to viewing eternity, where past, present and future merge. A communion, a union results (in yoga it's called a union of the sun and the moon) with the eternal and universal Spirit, the Higher Power, your own higher power.

In union the spirits shake hands, touch tenderly. They are all together. They are one.

I experience bliss, eternal bliss.

I have experienced this again and again in my journeys through time. In journeys such as these, all hurts and trauma from the human experience melt away and I connect with an infinite spiritual sense of eternity, wholeness and peace.

A particularly powerful breath session can catapult me out of my body. All of time just seems to stand still, and I am the observer. It is not unlike looking into the night sky and seeing a universe without boundaries, timeless in the infinity of space. Light in the vast heavens originates from realities eons away, yet it congeals instantaneously in the upward gaze of this moment. This is a miraculous sensation. I am suspended in time and space, eternally. There are no limits.

I use this, my time travel, as my prayer, my deliverance from the tyranny of unexpressed emotions. As I do so daily, my burdens turn to joy. I discover and express love of, for and to myself. It is one of my favorite ways to pray and actively meditate. My emotional release nourishes me and frees me to give unbounded affection, compassion, and tenderness. It allows me to act and react in a human, kindly, and disciplined way toward all who surround me.

What were the circumstances and situations that enabled me to arrive at this state of consciousness? Where did I derive the faith that caused my journey to take shape and form? Who were some of the personalities instrumental in motivating the choice of my spiritual pathway? We now begin the story of my path, one I trust will elucidate the way for you.

Points To Ponder

Time travel can benefit each of us in our path to personal growth and healing. Consider:

- What wonderful experiences might await you as you explore and transcend the damage to your own emotional body?
- Have you the patience, persistence and perseverance required to participate in profound transformational processes?

I have used a number of processes, including Rebirthing, bioenergetic exercises, Primal Therapy and Peer Co-Counseling to move through and beyond my emotional limitations. I encourage you to find experienced facilitators who can assist you in your dynamic growth process. Names and contact information are given at the end of this book.

Four

My Parents

Mom and dad were lovable people. Unlike so many I know who weren't cared for as children. I was fortunate being born into an extraordinary, intensely affectionate family.

My Dad

My dad was precious to me, always there for me emotionally. I always felt that loving connection from him, a connection I never took for granted.

He was a tall man, perhaps six feet. Dark hair and eyes accompanied his wonderful sense of humor and inviting smile. 'Good-natured', my mother always spoke of him. Genuinely kind and personable, he loved reading and singing.

Dad was a hard worker. His father had been a cooper. As a maker of wooden drums and barrels, grandpa had instructed his wife's brothers in the skilled craftsmanship of the cooperage business. Soon after, his brother's-in-law seized control of operations. Subsequently, my father's employment was tied to these cousins.

He drove a truck, which meant loading and unloading steel drums. He painted the steel drums he hauled in it, drums laden with chemicals from New Jerseys' oil companies. Physically, the job was murderous, though he claimed to enjoy it. I believe he knew all along that it was killing him.

A torn muscle bulged from the burly torso of his heavy frame. A sorry souvenir of years spent hoisting and carrying chemical drums without a mechanical lift. Everything about him was bigger than life, and indestructible. I always thought of him as the strongest man in the world, but looking back, I see that he had weaknesses as well. His addiction to sugar was overshadowed only by his two or three pack per day cigarette habit.

I remember his hands-callused, crusty, hard. Shaking always. The shaking begin as a child, he told me, the day scalding water scared his flesh to numbness. He never outgrew this fear or the feeling of helplessness the experience engendered.

I loved his undying availability to me, despite his impairments. He suffered from kidney and heart disease as well as emphysema. Unlike my Mother, Dad always had a solid grasp of reality.

He was hospitalized at the age of fifty-nine.

My parents felt families should care for their own and never believed much in doctors. Knowing this, his surgeon asked me to assist the implant of a pacemaker to help Dad's heart maintain its natural rhythm. I stood close by the surgical table holding my father's hand while the doctor performed the procedure. The local anesthesia seemed useless and Dad suffered tremendously. The thick nails of his massive hands penetrated my skin. With each wince of pain, I stood by faithfully, never letting go.

The procedure did not go well. After thirty-minutes of trying, the doctor finally gave up. The procedure failed.

My dad's hand relaxed, and I fainted briefly from the terror of witnessing this course of events. He passed away shortly after. The doctors claimed the final cause of death as emphysema.

His passing devastated me emotionally. He'd been tender and caring. I recalled his care for me while my mom was hospitalized; how he'd troubled himself speaking Yiddish to my aged grandmother.

My grief had taken on enormous proportions by the time my Dad's casket was finally lowered into it's grave. Using Primal Therapy as a release, it took at least four or five days for the heaviness in my heart to begin diminishing.

I thanked God for knowing how to process my grief. The release from deep within cleared the way for my inner strength to begin flowing. My life force increased, as I gained a greater sense of security and a sounder connection with life.

I recall thinking my dad would have been proud of me.

The release enhanced my contact with Spirit, and with *his* spirit. I felt his presence then, as I do now. It is an uncanny, yet comforting, sensation to know he watches over me. I am safe.

On Father's Day I attended Unity Church. The minister spoke about his relationship to his own father, and his words allowed me to release even more and to continue long after my departure.

I felt the terror and grief of my dad's death begging for release while listening to Robert Frey's song, 'Opening One's Heart to Love', I began my circular breathing exercises to connect with my deep-seated sadness and fear. As I did, the natural, emotional and physiological release began again. I gave thanks.

My Mom

I've always loved my mom. How could I help it? She always did her best for me, even though her history of nervousness kept us physically and emotionally separate. Her affection was expressed by a caring attitude.

She was a product of the Great Depression. The insecurity of that period negatively impacted the stability of millions of people, and left my mother nervous and subject to frequent loss of control. I always had a hard time expressing myself in her presence, and thus suppressed my thoughts or feelings in apprehension of her reactions. Only through the use of the Breath Work and Rebirthing have I been capable of releasing my fears relative to her.

Mom is alive and well today and is wonderfully supportive. I recently asked her to assist me in one of my breath sessions. I honor her hard work that day!

I took a young woman named Donna to a breath workshop not long ago. Very bright, Donna appeared troubled. She had been isolated for quite some time with nervousness similar to my Mother's. She had a tendency toward hysteria.

My intuition told me Donna and I could help each other. Because of her illness she talked constantly in hyper-animation, which frightened me. Her anxiety made it difficult to help herself, much less others. This similarity to my mom triggered strong fear, and I knew that working with her could help me overcome my troubles regarding abandonment.

No sooner had I started a breath session with Donna than I found myself agonizing emotionally. Finally, I reached an overwhelming sensation of grief. Again and again I repeated "I was so frightened! I was so frightened! I loved her so much!" The misery spewed forth in great bursts of energy. I connected to the core of the suffering. The process continued for quite some time. Afterwards, I felt more at peace, I was aware however that more needed to be released.

This provided an opportunity to learn non-attachment to hysteria, an arduous task. But through the aid of the Rebirthing, Primal Therapy and Healing Breath, not impossible! Donna continued accompanying me to breath sessions every week, as I toiled to desensitize and dissociate from my pattern of fearful reaction. I made tremendous progress releasing huge amounts of fear, and reinforcing my immunity against the effects of hysteria. I surrendered irrevocably. This was truly the path to wellness!

This emotional work enabled me to differentiate Donna from her illness, resulting in my greater sense of empathy for her.

One cannot help but admire the tenacity of the human spirit.

I accomplished the goal of freeing myself from fear of my mother's hysteria, but the stigma of our separation from my birth persisted.

Another Rebirthing session. I engaged in time travel, through circular breathing:

This session found I had internalized anger associated with my inability to control others behavior. The memories of my mom and the rejection that perceived by my infant self seized my mind. As in the past, I relived my grief and frustration at being devoid of control.

My lips echoed the words "I need! I need!" A shrill scream emanated from the pit of my stomach. She was never there when I really needed her! Unable to control her behavior, I internalized my anger, and fear.

This breathing session revealed that I continued to live in a self-defeating pattern. My feelings of helplessness with current situations, whereby people broke their agreements or failed to fulfill commitments to me, triggered the distress response of my infant within! I was responding to this frustration, his fear, and his sorrow.

It was time to take charge and eliminate self-inflicted pain. It was time to grow up. Connecting with my feelings of grief, I released them until at last I realized that my inability to control my environment resulted in my deprecating behavior. I'd been creating my own misery based upon a lifetime of conditioned responses and not even been aware of it!

Ultimately cognizant of what I'd been doing, I used this release session finding the strength to choose a different path. The realization that I could now choose my reactions in every environment extended me freedom from the responsibility for things I couldn't control. I could make healthier choices for myself. More importantly, I began entertaining healthier attitudes toward the people who I'd formerly attempted to control.

Points To Ponder

I found a variety of personal growth activities useful in dealing with the separation caused by my mother's chronic nervousness and my father's death.

Consider the following questions:

- How did your mother and father impact your life?
- Have you experienced losses relative to your parents that might be relieved by the use of such activities?
- What situations trigger your feelings of loss? Have you encountered people who you identify similar emotions with?
- Can you be empowered by strong feelings derived from past distresses?
- Is control an issue for you? Can you trace it back to birth or early childhood trauma? Is it time to let go of the need to control others' behavior?
- Can you connect spiritually with loved ones who have passed away?
- Can you imagine securing empowerment from a loved one 'on the other side'?

Five

A Journey of Faith

It is sometimes strange to consider the chain of events seemingly ordained for delivering us to a state of wholeness. On my journeys, I have met so many, friends/people, supposedly by accident, which have nurtured, sustained and encouraged me. I don't believe in accidents. I am sincerely grateful to them. Each who has come and gone has left a lasting impression, a gift that helped to build my faith and self-assurance.

It was springtime in New York City, 1971. My college drama class was producing a play about life in San Francisco. Our teacher (this may have been her first production) had orchestrated a musical scene. I walked on-stage, make-up freshly done. I stared into the audience, locking eyes with a lovely Philippine woman seated toward the front of the theater. She was exquisite and I was lured by her radiant smile... Her long, black hair glistened in the dim light while her sculpted eyes danced warmly across the subtle features of my own. She pursued me.

Her name was Ruth. Speaking Tagalong, English, and French, I admired her intelligence and her sensitivity, her vulnerability.

Moreover, she was tough. Wise in the ways of the world. She walked the streets of New York, with undaunted authority and awareness.

"Men are always following me," her eyes teasing. "I turn on them, like this," she scowled, executing an abrupt about-face, and "I chase them away." She laughed, and I joined in, delightedly.

I loved being physically and emotionally touched by her passion.

"I want to buy a motorcycle," she declared one day. "I've been shopping for one." "See how I look in my helmet?" Admittedly, the picture was stunning. In my mind, I saw images of her riding a Harley Davidson Chopper, her hair flowing in the wind.

Her childlike innocence made her vulnerable. The playfulness of our loving friendship made it special. Above all, she was emotionally supportive when I was in need. My anxiety peaked and I grew desperately fragmented.

Tortured by the hysteria echoing from the emotional peril of my childhood home life, the demands of my final year at Bernard M. Baruch College took on overwhelming proportions. Forever on edge, I found it impossible to relax or enjoy my studies. I needed a mother figure. I needed security.

I located a therapist near Columbia University, New York and began seeing her twice weekly. She was accepting of me. Following the third month of therapy, she admitted her non-professional interest in/with me. I was shocked. *This* was not supposed to happen.

I realized how fortunate I was to have a concerned female role model. I knew my mother loved me, but I'd never connected with her due to my fears regarding her instability.

Yet, I felt my therapist's love. It was dear and enabled me to complete my last year of school.

Ruth had a friend at Columbia University, Diane, who befriended me as well. We spent countless hours in each other's company. It was glorious, and I enjoyed their companionship.

In the summer of 1971, Diane accepted a summer internship with Mobile Oil of Holland, and Ruth went to visit her. Upon finishing my first summer of graduate school, they invited me to visit them in Amsterdam. I was soon on a plane to Holland.

Ruth had fallen in love with the City of Amsterdam, and I caught her enthusiasm. The lovely Dutch homes looking out over narrow canals made an endearing impression on these two idealistic young visitors.

Ruth and I decided to tour Paris and Rome. It was wonderful to be traveling together, sharing new experiences! We shared affection with each other as we explored the wonders of two great cities. The sights and sounds of antiquity spoke deeply, impacting my understanding. Unfortunately, Ruth had other demands on her time and could stay only a few days. I chose to remain in Rome a few extra days at the Salvation Army Hotel.

The hotel couldn't have been more appropriately named, for truly I felt in need of some 'salvation'. My continual anxiety was more than I could bear, and it didn't help that I inadvertently locked myself out of my room the first day and had to break the lock to get back in. How would I repair it? I needed a hammer and other small tools.

I knocked on the door of the room across the hall. To my surprise, the resident possessed a fully operative hammer! I repaired the lock on the door and returned the hammer to my friend, the Good Samaritan.

Jacob was a Hassidic Jew from the United States who had come to Rome to learn the Italian language. He was kind enough to show me around Rome and its beautiful suburbs, and we soon became steadfast friends.

Jacob was a holy man, a wanderer in search of himself, a seeker of God.

"That's why I'm here learning Italian," he told me. "Learning a second language is helping me find myself."

It was Jacob who first introduced me to the Spanish Steps. The steps must have been very, very old. They were a meeting place for peoples from around the world. Something strange happened when we visited those steps. They took on a spiritual significance for me. It was here that I would begin a life-changing journey to connect with my human and spiritual roots.

Jacob encouraged me to begin this journey.

"You should consider embarking on a pilgrimage to the Holy Land," he suggested. "You will learn so much about yourself by going back to your Hebrew roots!" His words still ring in my heart.

I had a few things to wrap up stateside before I could begin a pilgrimage to Israel. I needed to take some decisive action, so I returned to Manhattan to take a leave of absence from NYU and begin my quest for self. I wasted no time and returned to Rome where I purchased a rail ticket to the Italian port of Brindisi. Before my train departed I visited the Spanish Steps once more. To my surprise I met Jacob there. How fortuitous!

"I can hardly believe you're actually doing it!" he cried, hugging me and kissing my cheeks. "Please, have no fear, all will go well with you! You are on a blessed journey to the depths of your soul." His certainty was reassuring and inspiring.

The twenty-four hour journey from Brindisi to the Greek port of Patras passed uneventfully. The beautiful Adriatic Sea whispered its message of faith to me as the ferry passed islands suspended like links of chain on a bridge. The voyage from Patras to the port of Haifa, in the State of Israel, was heavenly. I slept like a baby aboard ship; free from the anxiety that kept me sleepless most nights.

Was it the sound of the sea rocking the ship like a secure cradle that brought me such peace or was it Jacob's assurance of faith in my journey that had taken hold of my spirit?

Points To Ponder

Foreign travel entailed risks that placed me in contact with those who planted the seeds of encouragement on my spiritual journey.
Consider the following:

- Have you begun your spiritual pathway?
- What will motivate and sustain you to begin and persevere with your own self-discovery?
- Do you have an idea of the nature of your spiritual direction?
- What emotional risks are you consciously willing to take to further your growth?

Six

Living in Israel and Scandinavia

"When you visit Israel you must live in a kibbutz," Jacob had prescribed. "Living and working in a foreign country will enhance your personal and spiritual growth. There is much you can learn about yourself in an environment vastly different from the place where you were raised."

"I've never been a Hebrew scholar," I lamented. "How will I get by?"

"Don't worry, there are plenty of Israelis who speak English. But learn as much of their language as you can—it will help you to see life from their perspective. I know you will find it spiritually significant to connect with your Hebrew roots. And you *must* have the experience of living on a kibbutz."

"What's it like?"

"It's a community of people who live together in a nurturing and sharing environment."

"Sounds good."

"Well, I can't guarantee you'll enjoy it— life in such a community can be a positive experience for everyone or a distressing one, depending upon the attitudes of the people and the circumstances of the community. But it's an experience you must have."

His words were uppermost in my mind as I began my journey to the State of Israel. I met a young Canadian named Jerry aboard the ferry from Patras to Haifa. Jerry seemed easygoing, and it was a joy to have him as a friend and traveling companion. We decided to find a kibbutz in the country where we could both reside.

I felt truly blessed to arrive in the State of Israel. My grandfather had always prayed about returning there. Perhaps I was realizing it for him.

In the summer of 1971 Jerry and I embarked on a journey to the Kibbutz Revivim, a community of four or five hundred people situated forty kilometers south of Ber Shiva in the northern Negev desert. Along the way our bus made frequent stops to pick up Bedouins who emerged as if by magic out of the desert shadows. These desert nomads were dressed in long robes, quite a contrast to our European dress.

I had come to Kibbutz Revivim to ground myself, to find myself.

Just outside the kibbutz stood a grove of trees where hundreds of ravens would congregate. The oasis seemed to have a sinister quality understood only by its winged inhabitants. They made me think of Edgar Allen Poe's poem, 'The Raven'.

Trips outside the kibbutz to biblical sites in the desert and the surrounding cities enabled me to connect with the timeless spiritual quality of the area. One night we undertook a trip to Mount Sinai, traveling through a dry riverbed where we slept under an endless expanse of stars. The Milky Way seen from the desert floor seemed to transcend all time and space, and we felt insignificant in comparison.

There were many volunteers on the kibbutz, from Denmark, Canada, Europe, and Asia. My twenty-third birthday was so very special! Forty-four volunteers from fourteen different countries celebrated it with me.

A number of the volunteers became romantically involved with each other, and I was no exception. I began a brief friendship with a lovely French girl. The kibbutz was a place for self-exploration and learning about oneself through relationships.

I practiced meditation and exercised by jogging. I worked in the orchard cheerfully, nurturing the peaches and learning irrigation techniques and systems. I attended the Hebrew school, where I began speaking the language.

I was assigned a kibbutz family. Daniel and Anna were in their 30s, both born in the new State of Israel. They were 'Sabras', sweet and gentle yet firm and assertive young people. They had a lovely daughter named Martha. Daniel was a member of the secret police and his wife Anna was an officer in the military. Daniel loved to drive a tractor as his streamlined Great Danes ran wildly beside its wheels.

Ruth flew in from New York City to visit me on the kibbutz. Her father worked for an airline, so she was able to catch a free flight to Tel Aviv. Though she loved me and I loved her, I told her I wasn't yet ready for a relationship. She understood, and after her visit we went our separate ways.

My year on the kibbutz ended all too soon. My next step in the journey was the city of Jerusalem, where I studied in a 'Yeshiva' (a Jewish religious school) for a month. This school was unique because its students were young men and women from all over the world who, like myself, had come in search of an identity. The Yeshiva didn't seem to have the answer for me, but I did enjoy listening to the spiritual fathers weave their ancient stories. This truly was a special experience.

One day I visited the medieval Castle Nimrod in northern Israel. The sun was low in the sky, and I decided to spend the night in the castle. A group of traveling physicians from the U.S.A., led by an Israeli, happened to be visiting the castle at the same time. The Israeli, realizing from my attire that I was from a kibbutz, invited me to travel with them. I accepted and joined the group. We visited Lake Keneret in the Galilee, where one of the physicians joked that Jesus had walked on the water. The other members of the group all broke out laughing.

I stayed silent. Somehow I connected spiritually with the holiness of that event, and thought it to be quite possible. After all, it was Jesus who had spoken at the local ancient synagogue near the lake! Truly, a spiritual presence seemed to envelop this area.

Despite their attitude, it was fun traveling with the doctors. Nevertheless I realized the time of my sojourn in the State of Israel was coming to an end.

I readied for my return to the U.S.A. While I knew my work with myself wasn't yet complete, I was unsure about the direction I was to take. The question on my mind that night was, "Where will my spiritual journey lead me next?"

My Introduction to Denmark

The ship left the port of Haifa, Israel, for the Greek Islands and its home port of Patras. We were three young men, all Jewish—an American, a Mexican and an Israeli, traveling together. We became friends and decided to disembark at the Greek Isle of Rhodes.

Once there, we began searching for a place to spend the night. We were tired, but eager to explore the city. My Mexican companion noticed two women seated close by and decided to pay his respects. My Israeli friend Eytan and I joined him.

We were delighted to meet these two lovely Danish women, Annika and Maria. Flirting with each other, we all developed a sense of rapport. Annika and Maria were nurses from Copenhagen, both open and delightful.

Annika was assertive and was clearly very much an 'in charge' nurse. Of medium build, she had rosy cheeks, green eyes, voluptuous breasts, and a beautiful dimple in her cheek. We liked each other from the start. She taught me some wonderful Danish words that translated to something like 'my drink, your drink, all the beautiful women drink'. We quickly became fast friends and companions.

Eytan and Maria hit it off equally well, and as a result we all spent seven wonderful days together enjoying the beauty of the Isle of Rhodes. We were particularly impressed with the 'Valley of the Butterflies', inhabited by thousands upon thousands of black and orange butterflies. Their presence empowered our spirits to take flight.

When it came time to part, Annika invited me to her place in Copenhagen. I didn't need much arm twisting to accept! I really liked her a lot and was in no hurry at all to return to the madness of New York City. A persistent recession gripped the U.S.A. at the time, and the prospect of driving a New York City taxicab to earn a living didn't inspire me much at all.

I followed Annika to Copenhagen, where we began to live together. Denmark was a very different social environment from the competitive one I had grown up in the U.S.A. Some five million people lived peaceably in this country, no bigger than the State of Nevada. Denmark is a social democracy, meaning that the government takes responsibility for its people. The Danish system of government attracted me, but I really wanted to live in the U.S.A.

Denmark offered no outward signs of people suffering. I saw no one living on the streets, down and out. I could not find the hopelessness I myself had experienced growing up on the streets of New York City. There was no 'bowery' (an economically depressed section of lower Manhattan where men and women struggled for survival). There was no one begging on the streets for money.

The society appeared to be very human. Employers felt no driving necessity to invalidate their employees. This was a watermark observation for me, because I had always been aware of my father's pain and murderous humiliation in the face of constant invalidation at the hands of the relatives who employed him. I loved my dad and had always wanted only good things to unfold for him. Sadly, this wasn't what happened.

My dad's problems with his family employment situation had predisposed me to expect work to be connected with pain. New York City had reinforced that expectation, but Copenhagen opened my mind to other alternatives: people can connect with their work in a positive, beneficial and meaningful way. It brought me a renewed sense of hope.

Points To Ponder

Traveling in a foreign country can be a tremendous assist on your quest to open to new possibilities and discover deeper truths about yourself.

Learning to speak Spanish, Hebrew and a Scandinavian language has been significant in my personal growth, as has my exposure to the Latin and Greek terms used in medical terminology. Learning phonics has helped me to anchor myself with sound. I believe this to be essential as a foundation for self-discovery.

'Alma' means 'soul' in Latin and Spanish. It has been said, "With the learning of each language an additional soul is created."

Consider the following:

• How might living in a foreign country enhance your personal and spiritual growth?
• What ethnic and spiritual roots might you find it helpful to connect with?
• What could you learn about yourself in an environment vastly different from the one in which you were raised?
• How could you benefit spiritually from learning another language?
• What advantage might there be in seeking gainful employment in a foreign country?

Seven

Annika

The windmills stretch out their arms to nurture the wind that blows across the fields, woods and hills of Denmark's Island of Bornholm, where sugar beets and strawberries thrive in perpetual abundance. The old castle stands majestically in its age-old glory, and the Lutheran churches serve as reminders of the people's seafaring past. Lilies of the Valley adorn the meadows, and buttercups smile in the soft breeze that moves them gently in their communion with the sunlight. Wild berries grow on bushes along lanes and hidden pathways. Cows roam aimlessly in the pastures. Swallows weave their playful patterns through the barns and out into the cloudless blue skies.

Nature seemed to be in an endless state of celebration when I came to Bornholm in the summer of 1972. Wild jackrabbits abounded. Migrating birds of all kinds used the lighthouses mounted on the tip of the island to rest between the legs of their journeys. Artists would come from all over the world to create their reflections of the island's awe-inspiring beauty. The cod were an easy catch, requiring only a hook and no bait.

The long summer days were mind-altering, a dramatic contrast to Denmark's winter darkness. The short but spiritual summer nights brought cool respite from the days' blinding sun. I learned it had long been a tradition during midsummer for virgin Danish maidens to open their wings and be penetrated by their chosen lover. Lovemaking unfolded very naturally here, free of the inhibitions of big city life. Schnapps and Danish brews flowed in abundance. On the downside, my nose was continually assaulted by the stench of vomit, a sour souvenir of young men and women's nightlong drinking.

Annika had invited me to Bornholm to meet her family. Her father was a Danish plantation owner. Her mother was a Finnish city-dwell-ing woman, yet somehow very different from the women I grew up with in New York City.

The island was off the East Coast of Denmark, a good four hours from Copenhagen. We traveled three and a half hours by ferry to reach it, and then an additional twenty-five minutes south to the village where Annika's family had their farm.

Annika was of the earth, a Danish farm girl. The earth had nurtured her, shaped her personality. She was practical, genuine, nurturing, tenacious and filled with the Creator's passion to celebrate and enjoy life. She was domineering, yet in no way a mean woman. She was a good and caring human being seeking a man. We were good prospects for each other. Timing is everything.

When we met she was employed as a nurse in a long-term care clinic; she later accepted employment as a supervisor over a facility for patients with tuberculosis. I respected her greatly, admired her ability to maintain a cheerful attitude with long-term care patients.

 Neither her instincts nor her impulses admitted of doubt or reservation. Unaccustomed to self-examination, she seemed uncomfortable whenever I suggested she look closely at her own behavior, thoughts or feelings. She was reliable and self-confident, the embodiment of feminine energy embracing life with zestful self-empowerment. I could not help but love her with passion. I considered myself fortunate that she loved me as well.

She was always prepared for battle with her father. She loved him but deplored his traditional attitudes toward women. She would speak up in defense of her mother, driving her point home in no uncertain terms with a quick, decisive tongue.

David, her father, a tall, angular man with blue eyes and balding hair, was a born farmer. His ancestors had come to the island in the Bronze Age. He liked playing chess, and was an avid reader. Although he read books about life in what he refereed to as 'the outer world', he left exploration and curiosity to others; he was always aware of his limitations. The youngest of six siblings, David was sensitive to life, in touch with its creative power. He'd never been comfortable with women, yet he firmly stood his ground when confronted by their liberal 'ideas'. His sisters had tended to be overbearing caretakers.

David had sold most of his animals by the time I arrived on the scene. He was employed as an island guide in semi-retirement and earned extra money from the labors of bees that constantly filled their honey cones. He invited me to assist him in relieving the honey-bees of the fruits of their instinctive labors. He cared about me, and I felt his love. I truly respected him.

Annika and her father spoke a strong island dialect, and I found it hard to understand what was being said at the dinner table. I often felt like an intruder in a world where I really did not belong. I felt scared, alone, splintered into a thousand emotional pieces strung together by thin, weak threads. Annika sensed how frightened I was, and I told her I was thinking of returning home. She encouraged me to stay.

"How can you survive in New York?" she would ask. "The 'Big Apple'? Such an evil place!" She loved me, and at times she almost became my surrogate mother.

I stayed, and in February of 1973 we were married in a town hall built in the 1400s. I got drunk on my wedding night. A Jew was marrying a Danish atheist? My mother would have had a nervous breakdown.

Our first year of marriage was difficult. There were no Americans for me to communicate with, and my feeling of isolation forced me to learn the Danish language at a breakneck pace. I undertook language classes at the university in Helsingor and began speaking Danish, but my anxiety was getting the better of me. I knew my days in Denmark were numbered.

Our village wasn't far from Sweden, and I often visited the city of Malmo there. People would never smile at one another on the streets in Sweden. The Swedes were generally stone-faced and withdrawn, and rarely spoke on the buses either. There must have been an unwritten rule encoded in the fabric of their society that perpetrated this overwhelming sense of coldness. I once heard someone blame it on the climate. A friend told me it could take over ten years to form a friendship with a Swede. How unlike Denmark and the multi-ethnic New York City, where people are generally open and friendly!

The state policy of socialism was strong in Sweden. The country had avoided both World Wars, and the society appeared incarcerated in its secure bubble. Nevertheless I did meet some warm and endearing Swedish people and was able to develop relationships there as well as in Denmark.

I was fortunate because of my marriage to Annika. She was open and friendly. I think she inherited her openness, her warmth and her ability to understand people from her Finish mother.

Darkness comes so early in the autumn in Denmark that it got on my nerves, created a strange sense of tension in me. My anxiety mounted, and I couldn't relax. I decided to take a class in **Transcendental Meditation**. It helped but not enough to still the longing for a way of escape. I continued to seek out alternative sources of help.

I met a teacher from California in Helsingor, and he introduced me to "Peer Co-Counseling," offering me my first experience with profound release of emotion.

My first Co-Counseling workshop took place on a cold winter day in a snow-covered village. I cried the whole weekend. The emotional release technique enabled me to relax for the first time in over a decade. I became an active participant in the Peer Co-Counseling community in Helsingor and Copenhagen. In the summer of 1973 I attended an international workshop in England with Mr. Harvey Jackins, the founder of Peer Co-Counseling, a mentor of enormous intelligence, wisdom and compassion. He taught us a process known as a 'Think and Listen' session, in which groups of people listen attentively while an individual brainstorms a problem without interruption.

It was inspiring to meet and experience people from different cultures raising their consciousness through emotional release and intelligent rational thinking. Our goal was to establish an international community of co-counselors in which individuals could find support for their evolving goals. I later became active in the counseling community, attending workshops in Massachusetts, Colorado, California, New York, England, France, Sweden and Denmark.

I returned to Denmark after the workshop with Mr. Jackins and began working with children at a local preschool. I found the work quite difficult at first but gradually adjusted to the environment.

Annika did her best to cope with my emotional ups and downs. She counseled me and supported me as best she could. It must have been quite difficult for her. She attempted Peer Co-Counseling as well but had some embarrassment around revealing herself. I prayed we would be able to experience personal and spiritual growth in our relationship together.

My emotional state was improving, but I didn't consider myself stable enough to start a family. I told Annika this, and shared with her my desire to return to the U.S.A. All this notwithstanding, Annika and I became pregnant. I returned to New York prior to my daughter's birth to find employment, intending to send for my family. Nothing worked according to plan. After months of unsuccessful job hunting I gave up and returned to Denmark, where I enrolled in school.

Lina was a completely lovable baby, precious, with blue eyes and chestnut brown hair. I felt very proud but found it difficult to adjust to the demands of fatherhood.

My anxiety mounted. Peer Co-Counseling helped, but was not strong enough to take me to the root of my difficulties and bring about deep healing. My marriage to Annika began to disintegrate, and we separated when Lina was two and a half. We continued to see each other for a while, but one day, seemingly out of the blue, Annika told me she no longer wished to pursue a relationship with me. She began meeting a man by the name of Tomas and became pregnant with his baby.

I fought for my family. I went to see Tomas at his place of employment, demanding that he stop seeing Annika. He willingly agreed but Annika became very upset. I became aware of Annika's pregnancy with Tomas and began to consider my daughter's well being.

Tomas, Annika, Lina and their new baby Peter began a new life together. Lina had to go through a period of adjustment. I was hurting deeply, but with the help and support of the Co-Counseling community I was able to keep my actions loving. My own attitude and Annika's were so very significant because they nurtured the well being of our daughter. Lina received loving support from all involved in our situation, and has grown to be a happy young adult. She is now studying in Honduras. I pray daily for her well being.

At about this time, I was introduced to a Primal Scream Therapy group that met in a member's basement to support each other through deep distress and emotional release. All those years of Peer Co-Counseling had primed me for this process, and it came naturally to me. I was able to relax and breathe deep into my terror, grief and rage, surrendering to whatever feelings needed to be expressed. There was a period of time when I experienced dramatic fear, and as a result started stuttering when I talked. I responded by continuing my release of this energy until my speech stabilized. I was starting to feel much safer with myself in the world. To my surprise, Denmark was becoming my home, and the Danish language had become my second soul. I felt a new joy in life. I had truly assimilated.

I finished my education in Denmark, received a teaching certificate, and began working as a bilingual English/Danish teacher in the preschools and elementary schools of Copenhagen. During this period I experienced my first among many primal birth releases. The feelings were huge, both powerful and painful. I released the terror of being unable to breathe because (as I perceived it) of the lack of space in the womb and birth canal. The support of several tenacious Danish primal practitioners was essential in helping me to connect with and power my way through those feelings of terror. I began to realize that terror, rage, grief, joy, bliss and love are only forms of energy, energy shared by all human beings, and that experiencing and releasing this energy is a natural part of life. I began to think of pain as an energy force. It was no longer a thing to be afraid of. I started to appear younger, look healthier and feel stronger. I realized I could nurture myself by dancing through some aspects of my pain.

My Swedish friend Lisa-Lott introduced me to the benefits of **Reflexology**. Reflex points in the feet connect to the heart, the major organs, the glands and the nervous system. When these points are stimulated, emotional blockages in the body are released. This practice helped me access and connect with feelings requiring release, feelings I processed by emoting them in Primal Therapy.

One day as I lay on the operating room table about to have two Danish physicians remove my wisdom teeth, I actually started to laugh. I yawned, surrendering to the pain. The two physicians thought my behavior was strange but encouraged me to continue, aware that I was dealing effectively with the pain by releasing my feelings. I recuperated very quickly after the medical procedure.

Years later I underwent a surgical procedure performed on many athletes who over-train and develop a varicose vein in the scrotum. This surgery was very painful. I released my feelings by way of yawning and laughing in this situation as well. This made my body shake, hindering the surgeons in their work, so I stopped until the procedure had been completed. Once again the release of my emotions encouraged the healing process.

I have returned to Denmark on several occasions to visit my lovely daughter and my Danish friends, and Annika came to visit me in the U.S.A. with Lina in 1983 as well.

Healing Practice: Peer Co-Counseling

Peer Co-Counseling is an emotional release processes useful for focusing specifically on recovering from painful emotional and physical experiences or conditions. Co-Counseling partners help each other release pent-up emotions through animated speech, chattering, shaking, hot and cold sweats (for fear), tears (in relationship to grief), and perhaps beating a pillow or making angry noises (for anger).

During and subsequent to this form of release and emotional discharge there is a re-evaluation of painful experiences. Once adequate emotional release is achieved the participant is left without the painful experience but retains the memory of the situation and circumstance along with newly gained insights. I have successfully practiced Peer Co-Counseling for twenty-eight years all around the world: in the United States, in Europe, in Scandinavia, and in Israel. It is a proven performer and a valuable tool for gaining insight and healing. I have maintained a seventeen-year Peer Co-Counseling relationship with a New York Co-Counselor on a bi-weekly basis by telephone. Our growth has been significant because of the trust that has grown from the depth of our sharing over the long term.

Healing Practice: Primal Scream Therapy

Primal Scream Therapy is a well-known method developed in the 1970's by Arthur Janov. We use the scream to release distressful energy. It works! Through the combination of Primal Scream, Breath Work, Peer Co-Counseling, and Tae Kwon Do or bioenergetic methodologies I have been able to fully release my emotions. The result has been a total catharsis leading to a sense of peace and dynamic spiritual growth.

Healing Practice: Transcendental Meditation

Meditation is a wonderful process I use proceeding and/or subsequent to a breathing session. I have had deeper, more profound meditations subsequent to my breathing sessions than when I have practiced meditation by itself. The combination of these two has helped me find greater peace within myself. As Joseph P. Thompson has said, "Real glory comes from the silent conquest of ourselves." **Transcendental Meditation**, brought to this country by Maharishi

Mahesh Yogi, is a particular form of meditation I learned in Scandinavia. This practice makes use of a mantra (sound) to focus the energy and help release anxiety.

Healing Practice: Reflexology

Reflexology is a form of bodywork practiced on specific parts of the body containing 'reflex points' relating to all parts of the body. The work stimulates the immune system and brings about healing. I became acquainted with **Foot Reflexology**, in which points on the feet are stimulated, in Sweden, where my dear friend Lisa-Lott performed several sessions on me.

Points To Ponder

Peer Co-Counseling and Primal Therapy have been of immense help to me in resolving issues close to my heart. Consider the following:

• What areas of your life could be helped by such methodologies? Are you in a relationship, going through a divorce, making changes in your life style, adapting to a different culture, or in some other transitional state in which these methodologies might be helpful?
• What personal growth challenges and opportunities are presenting themselves now in your life?
• If you were to pursue those opportunities, what could you do to increase the likelihood of their enhancing your life?

Eight

New York City

I was unaware of the degree of emotional adjustment my accultura-
tion to Scandinavian life had required of me. Returning to New York
City in the fall of 1979 was like being reborn into a new world of
thinking, feeling, and interpersonal relations with behaviors I had become unaccustomed to. After weeks of searching, I finally found employment with the Health Department's immunization program, a
job I held for two and a half years.

It was on returning to New York that I made an interesting discovery: in my travels between the U.S.A., Scandinavia and Israel I had
found jet lag to be a problem. But on the flight home I discovered that
releasing my feelings through circular breathing allowed my body to
make a quick transition to present time. Perhaps the breathing stimulated production of endorphins in the brain? Whatever the reason, I
felt better and my attentiveness was dramatically heightened.

I continued my Rebirthing and Healing Breath Work in New York,
as well as Peer Co-Counseling and Primal Therapy. By now I had
enough experience and confidence to conduct successful primal sessions on my own, so I was able to save myself a great deal of time
and money. I became quite proficient in counseling myself, connecting with my emotions and releasing them through the use of positive
affirmations said with conviction in the silence of my mind. The
combination of all of these methodologies helped me readjust
quickly to my new environment.

I went on a series of retreats to a Buddhist monastery in
Woodstock, New York, poised at the crest of Mead Mountain. Here I
experienced profound periods of meditation and chanting.

In 1983 my friend Jonathan introduced me to Ananda Ashram, a blessed retreat at the foot of the Catskill Mountains in the town of Monroe. The on-site spiritual leader, Dr. Mishra, was from India, and I had trouble understanding his speech. Not that I minded—the loving kindness and human charity that emanated from his heart were ample compensation for the investment of concentration required to understand his spoken words.

The ashram was a haven for me, a place where I could retreat from the stresses of New York City. I visited on a regular basis, often climbing to the top of a hill to watch a hawk circling the valley below. I swam in the lake, rested under the trees and enjoyed the pleasant views. A variety of metaphysical practitioners frequented the retreat. Psychics, Sufi masters, talented dancers, musicians and martial arts practitioners visited regularly. It was here that I became acquainted with **Sufi Dancing**, an uplifting spiritual form of folk dancing I found easy to learn and most enjoyable. We danced in a circle to live music, making eye and heart contact with each new partner. I also had my first experience of Japanese **Shiatsu Massage** at the ashram, from a highly intuitive practitioner with a thorough understanding of the interrelationships between body, mind and spirit.

I owed all these new experiences to my Peer Co-Counselor friend Jonathan, a short, stocky man of 62. Jonathan was quite bright, with some interesting idiosyncrasies. For one thing, he liked collecting old clothes. His collection of ties dated back to the 1930s. Once when I visited him at his home he trotted out his collection of ties and shoes. There were boxes of old clothes everywhere, with labels indicating the month and year he had acquired them. He loved showing off his collection of socks from the '40s and the '50s and bizarre cartons filled with plaid shirts that had long ago surrendered their buttons.

Jonathan was clock-wise. He always arrived on time. I don't believe he was ever late for anything. "I was born exactly on time," he told me. He would eat at precisely the same hour every day. He would brush his teeth twice a day at exactly the same time. He and his girlfriend Dana made love at 11:30 p.m. on the same two nights every week. He would visit the same museum once a month, purchase clothes at the same stores every week, and go to bed at precisely the same minute every night. There was no end to his precision.

Jonathan was a sweet, kind, intelligent man, a genuine human being. I loved him dearly. New York City produces the most uniquely multi-faceted and fascinating human beings! The coping mechanisms necessary to maintain one's viability in a city of its intensity produce personalities of the most dramatic kind. You can find the very best and the very worst of personalities on the city streets, profoundly human and inhuman characters. I don't think I ever experienced a dull personality there.

I left the immunization program and took a job with the Communicable Disease Bureau, where I worked in all five boroughs and thirteen clinics of the city of New York conducting extensive and intensive interviews with patients who had contracted a variety of sexually transmitted diseases. I learned a great deal about the sexual and non-sexual lifestyles of heterosexuals, transsexuals and homosexuals.

I interviewed individuals who were infected by the penicillinase-producing Neisseria Gonorrhea, a strain of gonorrhea resistant to penicillin. Since the disease was expensive to treat, the Bureau made a major effort to track down those who might have been exposed to it with the goal of reaching their sex partners before the incubation period ended and the disease took hold. This job was seldom dull. It was sometimes embarrassing, though, as it was the time I mistook the father of an infected patient for his gay lover.

The job brought me into contact with drug addicts, prostitutes and pimps. We respected all human beings and did our best to refrain from making judgments about their chosen fields of employment. The work was not without its risks; one night as I was leaving a clinic I was attacked by two young men as I reached for my auto keys. Fortunately I had studied Karate and was able to protect myself and frighten them off.

During my last six months in this job my thoughts of syphilis, herpes, and AIDS began keeping me awake at night. Again, I used the emotional release techniques to help me through the most difficult of times. I held onto this job for as long as possible but finally I realized it was time to move on.

Healing Practice: Sufi Dancing (Dances of Universal Peace)

Sufi Dancing (Dances of Universal Peace) is a tradition of loving circular dances in which the dancers maintain eye contact as they greet one partner after another as they travel around the circle. I have found Sufi Dancing to be spiritually uplifting and truly loving in its expressions towards and contact with others. It is in contacting others that I have come into closer communion with my own self-discovery.

Healing Practice: Affirmations

Faith in others proceeds from your faith in yourself. **Affirmations** are specific statements you make to yourself to bring about change in your belief system and behavior. It has been said that you will be unable to trust the words of anyone until you learn to trust your own; speaking your highest truth in front of a mirror can be an effective way to empower and develop your spiritual self. Never underestimate the power of watching you speaking to you!

For best results, phrase your affirmations in the present tense, from the point of view of already having achieved whatever it is you're after. For example: "I am financially abundant and enjoy radiant health." Be as specific as possible.

Healing Practice: Shiatsu Massage

Shiatsu is a Japanese form of body massage in which a practitioner treats an individual along specific 'meridians' in the 'subtle body', moving the energy called '*ki*', the Japanese word for the life force that sustains all activity of the spirit, mind, and body. The recipient can be sitting or lying in various positions while the practitioner uses the power of their thumbs, hands, fingers, forearms, knees and feet to massage the torso and release energy blocks. The thumbs are the body part of use by the traditional practitioner.

Points To Ponder

Life seems to bring us one stressful situation after another. Consider the following question:

• What strategies have you found helpful in dealing with physical displacement symptoms such as jet lag, adjusting to a new environment, or managing job stress? Might Peer Co-Counseling and Primal Therapy be of use to you in these situations?

• "I think well of myself" is an excellent affirmation I have used effectively to put a halt to negative and self-defeating thoughts. Could this simple positive affirmation help you? Please feel free to use it!

Nine

Love and Co-Dependency

I was engaged for a time in a 'co-dependent' relationship with a woman I cared for deeply.

Lynn was joyful and enthusiastic, and she had a great sense of humor. A craft-worker, she was creative and meticulous. She loved bowling and water skiing. And food! Her favorite food was a T-bone steak with mashed potatoes and gravy.

We met in a yoga class in Los Angeles—she, the child of an anxious American professional, and I, son of an anxious Jewish mother. Both our families had suffered economic scarcity, and we'd both endured more than our fair share of physical illness. We were both dealing with abandonment issues from childhood—hers had left her angry, mine had left me terrified.

Ours was a rocky relationship, with lots of ups and downs. We broke up several times over the two years we were in each other's lives.

The glue that held us together in a loving space was a counseling process known as the "Dyad Method." We also read and practiced exercises from *Getting the Love You Want*, a book by Harville Hendricks, Ph.D.

The Dyad Method was particularly helpful because it gave each of us a chance to express our thoughts and feelings while the other listened. We weren't required to try to fulfill each other's needs, only to give ourselves a chance to view each other's issues. As a result we experienced a continually developing empathy and increased level of caring for each other.

Our love grew, and we learned how to be patient and empathetic with each other and ourselves. The relationship was filled with important lessons for us both.

Lynn's emotional scars from a previous abusive relationship made physical intimacy confusing. Although I always tried to be caring when I touched her, she would often pull away at my slightest touch. I cared deeply for her, and we had our moments of pleasurable intimacy, but there were times when her pain was too much for me and I refused to be with her.

I was emotionally devastated when Lynn left with someone else. Betrayed again! Thanks to my training in emotional clearing, I realized Lynn's leaving had re-stimulated primal feelings of abandonment installed when my mother left me to go into the hospital right after I was born.

Using a combination of Healing Breath, Rebirthing, and Primal Therapy, I reconnected with and released old feelings of abandonment. It was not easy. My feelings about 'losing' Lynn were incredibly intense, but as I reconnected with my inner child and released my pain I experienced a new level of self-empowerment.

Lynn's relationships since our parting have not proceeded without problems. She contacted me recently, saying she'd like to start dating again. She was obviously quite confused. She told me she was unable to get over her infatuation with a guy by the name of John. She claimed she needed men to fulfill her needs. I had come to realize that our relationship, while it had been deeply loving, was also overly co-dependent and therefore destructive to both of us. For her sake as well as mine, I asked her not to call anymore. Setting my boundaries with her helped me shed the skin of co-dependency, and that has made me a healthier, happier person.

Nature, I believe, brought Lynn and I together to help us heal each other's wounds. I pray she will find herself. I send her light, love, and happiness whenever I think of her. Learning non-attachment with others while still maintaining a loving attitude takes a great deal of emotional and mental self-discipline. I used Peer Co-Counseling as well as the breath work, Tae Kwon Do and meditation to help me through the process. The peace I discovered, that of the inner child remains with me to this day.

The emotions of betrayal, abandonment, separation, being good enough, and being overly needy for warmth and tenderness nearly always accompany the ending of an intimate relationship. Once we learn how to be compassionate with these all-too-human feelings, we can release them at the very core of our being and reconnect with the joyous child within.

Recently a friend invited me to a singing class in which a group of seniors proudly expressed themselves independently or in pairs by singing. I mustered the courage to get up and sing. From my heart I sang a Scandinavian children's song filled with passion and joy. Afterward a gentleman approached me to tell me my song had given him an increased level of joy and a renewed connection with his childlike nature.

I was so happy to hear I'd helped him connect with his inner child. My experiences of pain and abandonment had empowered me to empower, encourage and give hope to a fellow traveler.

Why do human beings have controlling behaviors? The experiences of abandonment, separation and betrayal are some of the reasons. Trust is part of a human beings persona. When we get hurt experiences of fear, anger and sadness impact our ability to trust. The need to control can result. As we access, connect with, and release our hurt feelings, our trust for others returns. We free ourselves from the need to control others.

Healing Practice: The Dyad Method

The Dyad Method teaches listening attentively to another person as they relate their experiences in a given situation. The goal is to access and listen to their realm of consciousness and to understand how it influences their behavior. One soon learns that our perceptions of each other are not always correct, and that we often misunderstand the behaviors of others.

This counseling method involves several steps that create the space for individuals to experience compassion for each other and themselves.

Points To Ponder

Human beings are often faced with feelings of abandonment and betrayal at the end of a relationship. Consider the following:

- How might accessing and connecting with the distress associated with your own abandonment, separation, and betrayal experiences open doorways to reconnect with your inner child?

- How might reconnecting with your inner child be helpful to you?

Ten

Loneliness And Fear Of Loneliness

I am not alone in my sense of aloneness.

— Anonymous

Have you ever been lonely? Most of us have. And those of us who have don't exactly relish the idea of being lonely again.

People who live alone are often lonely, but so are people who live with their families. Loneliness and the fear of loneliness are devastating emotions shared by millions. They are the cornerstones of abandonment issues and co-dependency.

Our fear of loneliness may stem from birth, infancy, or childhood abandonment, or our separation from a loved one as an adult. Through the use of Rebirthing, Healing Breath, Primal Therapy, meditation and other methods, I have learned how to turn loneliness into an opportunity for finding greater peace and harmony in my periods of aloneness.

Having developed my ability to release these devastating parasitic emotions, I feel freer, more open and relaxed in my life, and happier maintaining my present life style as a single man.

This is an ongoing process. I take pro-active social steps in my life to be with others and participate in cooperative and constructive goals. This is very helpful. Having fun is important too. Equally important is the ability to learn the bliss of solitude and aloneness through consistent and effective release.

Cindy

Cindy was forty years old when I met her at a Breath workshop. She loved eating meat, and spoke in particular about her love of beef.

Though I am a semi-vegetarian, I loved being with her because of her wonderful laugh and smile and her effervescent sense of humor.

When she asked me if I'd like to exchange Reiki Healing work with her, I didn't have to think twice.

"I'd be happy to exchange with you," I said.

Reiki healing was a 'natural' for me. I learned how to use my hands to exchange a loving sensation and release accumulated distress in the body. I learned that light energy is so powerful that I don't even need to touch a recipient's body to radiate healing energy into it and heal emotional and physical trauma.

Cindy had been abused during her marriage of many years and wanted nurturing. We needed each other and were sensitive to each other's need to heal old wounds. It was a time of great healing for both of us.

Jane

Jane had moved from New Jersey to San Diego three years before I met her in a spiritual community in southern California, where she did a Rebirthing session for me. She had the most incredible brown eyes! She always wore these brown leather boots her dad had given her—I think she was addicted to those boots!

We saw each other at a variety of classes, and after a time we became friends. I asked her to a party, and that night we became loving friends.

On the first evening of winter Jane phoned me, frightened and anxious, one sentence running into another like boxcars in a train crash. I stopped her and acknowledged her state of being. "It's alright, Jane, I'm here for you. I'm here for you, as a loving friend," I assured her.

But I found it very hard to listen to her. Her words were stimulating my old feelings of fearfulness, and it hurt. I felt like running away. But I didn't run. Instead I stayed on the line and tried to stay linked to her, doing my best to put my own fear aside.

I was unsuccessful.

The next morning I woke up feeling a burning emotional and physical pain centered in my pelvic area. I began circular breathing in an attempt to release my fears.

I went on like this for about an hour, until finally I realized I needed to speak with Jane again and tell her pattern of speech triggered within me such a sense of insecurity it made me want to not talk to her at all. Although I felt uncertain about how to confront her with this truth, I knew I couldn't run from my fear. I picked up the phone.

As I stepped into my fear and opened myself up, making myself vulnerable to her, she actually heard me.

"Don't worry, Joel, I'm here for you, too," she assured me. "That was pretty courageous of you, to call me and tell me I was driving you nuts with my fears! I was about to pick up the phone and call you, and here you are calling me. Isn't that great? I'm here for you, I want to know what you're feeling."

That felt good.

"I was really quite frightened, you know." she went on. "I received a very troubling letter from my parents today, and I was apprehensive about telling you because I was afraid I would make you want to run away from me. I got so depressed thinking I might lose you...."

So, although she'd assured me that she was there for me, in reality I saw that she was looking for me to save her. She sounded wildly anxious, and once again I began to feel overwhelmed. I decided to do a breath session as soon as I hung up.

As I began my breath session the feelings of fear begin to well up from deep within my being. I was fearful of expressing myself. Afraid of being rejected for speaking up, for speaking out, for being articulate. Throughout my life I'd had a pervasive and chronic terror of saying or doing the wrong thing. Was it something I'd done that had made Jane fearful and anxious?

As I continued my circular breath, releasing my negative feelings, I began to feel more and more self-confident. I came to understand that my chronic fear of doing the wrong thing had its origin in my birth experience. Once I released this terror I was able to relax and feel comfortable, more self-assured in all my relations. I sensed a new strength. Of course I could speak out and stand up for myself!

Exhilaration!

I followed up the next day by practicing Tae Kwon Do and doing a Peer Co-Counseling session. Finally I knew I was ready to phone Jane and speak in a meaningful way to her, with a high degree of self-confidence. Feeling better about myself, I felt better about Jane, and our loving friendship continued.

It is interesting to note that Jane had a long history of physical abuse at the hands of men, as did Cindy and Lynn. Clearly, a pattern was emerging in my relationships with women. They were all in need, as was I, of a loving friend.

We were all in transition. Perhaps all we all needed was tender loving care for a season. I realized I had been in the rescuer role too long, and that it was my own chronic insecurity that catapulted me into that role.

It was important for my own mental health to put an end to all this rescuing and conquer my chronic need for nurturing. I needed to learn to nurture myself!

I've found my unfolding is a continual process. I continue to nurture my inner child even now! I am there with warmth and caring to protect him from ever again experiencing major trauma. I'm grateful for the loving friendships that helped bring me to this point.

Healing Practice: Reiki

Reiki (pronounced 'ray-key'} is the Japanese word for 'universal life' energy', a form of healing based on tapping into the unseen flow of energy that permeates all living things. Reiki sessions are powerful, yet gentle and nurturing. Clients remain fully clothed in their own comfortable, loose-fitting clothing to permit full relaxation. A soothing environment is provided. A Reiki Practitioner is trained to access and direct the universal life force energy to the client's body through a very light touch using approximately twenty standard hand positions or a hands-off technique. No rubbing or massaging is done. Sessions normally last an hour, though this may vary. I found Reiki sessions helpful in healing my arthritic knee.

Healing Practice: Tae Kwon Do

Tae Kwon Do is a Korean Martial Art. I've practiced Tae Kwon Do for twelve years and have found the series of stretching, cardiovascular activities and Martial Art forms to be very conducive to connecting with my physical and emotional power, especially in conjunction with Rebirthing. The stretching, cardiovascular, and martial art forms help in clearing any resistance that prevents accessing, connecting, and releasing stressful feelings.

Points To Ponder

Loneliness and the fear of loneliness frequently trigger states of depression. Consider:

- When have you experienced feelings of loneliness, or the fear of loneliness?
- Do you suffer from depression attributable to loneliness or the fear of loneliness?
- Have you found workable ways to transform these feelings? If not, do you think some of the methodologies I've used might be worth a try?

Eleven

Being Good Enough!

When your body aches, it's not necessarily easy to see that it may be offering you a gift. Yet it is—it is offering you an opportunity to learn something about yourself and make self-empowering changes.

I have learned that physical challenges often have psychological causes. They are often rooted in an indoctrinated set of rigid beliefs. The 'scarcity trauma' and chronic fear of 'not having enough' and 'not being good enough' are good examples of this. On February 6, 1998, I experienced a physical challenge that uncovered an unexpected source of empowerment in my life.

I felt pain coming from my lower back. I have a minor impairment there. Funny, how our tensions harbor in the more sensitized areas of the body! I began my circular breath. An overwhelming feeling of sadness swept over me, the old familiar sadness of having done something terribly wrong.

"I did something wrong by being born into the world! I hurt my mom by being born!" Such were my thoughts.

I suspected my pain was signaling the need for release of my chronic sense of guilt, fear, and grief. To counter this self-defeating belief, I began declaring otherwise.

"*I am a product of creation, and I believe I am good enough,*" I declared. As quickly as the negative feelings came up, I released them with the circular breath. I began saying to myself, "*I really am good enough. I really am good enough.*"

These positive affirmations helped me connect with and release my negative thoughts. It helped me even more to look into a mirror while making these positive statements about myself. Gazing into my own eyes, I was able to love myself more powerfully, creating a metamorphosis toward a positive thought pattern that would lead to a new and healthier identity.

I had learned that being consistent and effective in this practice is essential for a positive result. I had also learned that following an affirmation session with a more profound emotional modality, such as Peer Co-Counseling, Rebirthing, Healing Breath or Tae Kwon Do, could be helpful in reinforcing the positive effects of my affirmations. Follow-up, and following up on the follow-up, is essential to creating a new conscious reality. You have to be willing to do whatever it takes!

I released my sadness with tears and moved into a deeper state of reality and a new consciousness. Now my words were, *"I was* always *good enough!"* And in that instant I knew it was so. This was and remains a new state of reality and enlightenment for me.

On February 10, 1998, I again sensed a great deal of fear. The fear (false evidence appearing real) harbored as piercing pain in my pelvic area and as pressure in my head. I made an appointment to see my kinesiologist chiropractor that very morning, and he helped me by making adjustments that relieved these intense physical sensations.

The week ahead loomed large. I was scheduled for several job interviews and a presentation before a group of medical teachers.

My pain returned frequently during the day. Again and again I used breath work to release it and channel its energy into empowerment. Was my pain arising out of my fear, or did it have a physiological source? Intuitively I began to perceive that it was rooted in chronic distress. What was the nature of that distress? As I began the circular breath once again, fears came up and I began to release them. Miraculously, the pain in my pelvic area began to dissipate.

The symptoms returned a couple of hours later and I began my circular breath once again. Once again the intense fear and pain were released from my pelvic area and within my head.

This period of unemployment was particularly stressful for me. It triggered a major scarcity trauma from the lower levels of my unconscious, of which I became more and more aware as I continued to release my fears. When I was young, my mother had filled me with stories of her sad economic plight during the Great Depression.

I had felt sincere empathy for her, but of course I co
and be there for her to alter her situation. Her anxiety
had frightened me and caused me much grief. The affir
that mother, nurturing that little boy, right now! I (
nurturing that little boy, right now! I am in charge now!" helped to
calm my insecurities and return me to balance and self-confidence.

I decided to return to my chiropractor for a follow-up visit to determine the nature of my distress. I needed to know whether it was in
fact my fear that was causing my physical discomforts, or whether
there was some physiological source. My chiropractor explained that
one of my kidneys did need adjustment but that an imbalance in the
kidney region often signaled a high level of fear within the consciousness of human beings. He went on to suggest that relaxation would
occur when the fear was released from the pelvic region.

His diagnosis confirmed my intuition. My pain had been merely a
reflection of my fears. I was sure my present life situation reflected
my scarcity issue. That week I participated in several breathing sessions, a yoga session, two sessions with the chiropractor, Tae Kwon
Do sessions and a Jacuzzi, and documented my experience. My lower
back stopped hurting!

I found that some of my 'not good enough' feelings had come from
my affiliations with religious authorities who had been serving their
own self-interests—and seeking to control others. Over the years I
had come to believe in their system of control. By buying into their
dogma on an emotional level I had made myself deeply anxious. It
was my virtual enslavement to their controlling ideas and beliefs
about life that had triggered my feelings of inadequacy and subsequent lower back pain. This was a major realization for me. I used
these powerful affirmations to help me reclaim my own power: *"I*
choose life now! I live in the world fully and courageously now!"

Through this physically and emotionally challenging experience I
became impacted by a scarcity trauma and became acutely aware of
the effects religious teachings could have on a person's health and
well being. I have since made it a point to no longer allow the authori-
tarian doctrines of any institution to give me a sense of my not being
good enough or inadequate. I no longer buy into the guilt of a dog-
matic doctrine. I've taken charge. I've chosen a healthier perspective!

I had gained a new appreciation for the value of affirmations as
an assist to profound emotional release work. I have used the affir-

mations *"I have enough," "I know enough," "I am good enough," "I am enough"* and *"I do enough in the world" as* a teacher in the 'welfare to work' and 'GAIN' (Greater Avenues for Independence) programs. It has helped to change people's attitudes about themselves and created significant shifts in their self-identity.

Points To Ponder

I am convinced that our physical aches and pains, as well as our more serious illnesses, are often the result of stored emotions endeavoring to gain our attention. Consider the following:

- Do you have recurring aches and pains? Are you aware of the emotions underlying them?
- Do you have a way that works to release the emotions and get rid of the pain?
- Do you know how to find out what the underlying emotions are?
- Would you be willing to try some of the approaches I have found useful in this regard?

Twelve

My Career as a Teacher

Substitute Teaching Was a Headache!

When I first moved to San Diego, California, I took a sales position with a major insurance company.

I also acquired a teaching credential and found employment in local colleges and elementary schools. I enjoyed teaching adults, but the children were a challenge for me. I loved young people and had trained for two years as a pre-school teacher at a specialized Scandinavian school, yet I found some of the behaviors of my elementary school students difficult to cope with. Their shouting and screaming were constant reminders of my own past distress and threw me into a state of fearful anxiety.

My life as an elementary teacher provided me with ample reason to continue exploring and dealing with my own emotions. Substitute teaching I found particularly stressful; substituting in a variety of classes in a given week would give me migraine headaches. As far as I knew, I had not inherited a genetic tendency toward migraines. I do remember my mom experiencing some pretty severe backaches and headaches, but I don't believe they were classic migraines.

My migraines seemed to be related to stress. I discovered I could use the headaches as a spur to emotional, intellectual, and spiritual expansion, leading to greater personal growth and freedom. Stretching, engaging in cardiovascular activity, practicing the Tae Kwon Do forms and exercises and releasing energy through a Primal Breath session would relieve my migraines every time!

I also used the ancient Chinese Art of Acupuncture on many occasions to relieve stress accumulated in my throat because of blocked emotions associated with teaching, and to relieve the pain of osteoarthritis and carpal tunnel syndrome. Acupuncture opened emotionally blocked energy and allowed me to connect with, access, and discharge feelings. In addition, I used wrist exercises, ice and **Chinese herbs** to restore my body to balance.

Surviving Second Grade

Chaos reigned in the second grade classroom, even with four adults doing their best to provide some semblance of order. The regular teacher was clearly burned out, and the mentor teacher was overwhelmed. That left the aide and the part-time visiting teacher—me.

I often thought we could have used a therapist or ten.

How do you deal with twenty-one children in distress? These kids were locked into a cycle of provoking aggressive reactions in their peers and doing what they could to defend themselves. They had little attention for learning.

Duane and Isaiah were disturbed little boys. I watched as they jockeyed for position in the class, doing their best to establish their territory. When the mentor teacher confronted them about their behavior they lashed out at her. She was appalled, and asked me to take both of them to see the principal.

The two boys became very upset. I reached down and took them gently by the hand, and we walked out of the classroom. Their fear touched me, and I knelt down and asked them if they would like a hug. They stepped into my arms on either side and began to cry profusely.

"No one is going to hurt you," I assured them. "I'm here for you. You are loved. Neither of you are bad boys. There's nothing to be afraid of. You're fine just as you are." I repeated my assurances with feeling, again and again. I whispered in their ears, "I understand how it feels. It's okay to feel that hurt."

The boys continued to sob on my shoulder. "I am here for you," I continued to repeat. These words seemed to have a positive effect on both of them.

Realizing that the enormous distress of their personal lives was affecting their behavior in the classroom, I didn't feel additional punishment was the answer. As I continued soothing their emotions, eventually their tears abated. Giving them an opportunity to release their emotions seemed to help them to trust—first themselves, and then me as well. In the end they both felt like cooperating with me.

"I want to tell the teacher I'm sorry!" Duane declared. Isaiah nodded in agreement. "Me too."

I believe the key factor with children is to establish a firm and compassionate loving presence for them in a genuine and empathetic way. This takes human skill that no 'book learning' can teach.

There is so much that can be done in the schools to help small children who are confused by a chaotic adult world. Teachers and counselors need to be sensitized emotionally by becoming aware of their own emotional issues and working through them.

Los Niños Del Señor Vorensky

Ruben was an aggressive, disruptive, frightened child. Marie was sweet, but slow to catch on. Rosa suffered from malnutrition. Blanca, who had previously been in an all-English class, resented her mother for enrolling her in a first grade Spanish class. Patricia was a daydreamer. Carlos was constantly falling asleep in class. Roberto was always moving his chair as his focus shifted from one thing to another. Karen had a tendency to be controlling of other students. Joel bit his nails and scratched his skin. Marisol exhibited acute anxiety and could be obnoxious. Getting the attention of twelve Mexican-American first graders designated as victims of attention deficit disorder ('ADD') was a daily struggle.

My job was to teach them to read in Spanish using a phonics approach. I had accepted a seven-month contract, the toughest teaching assignment I had ever encountered. I had never studied Spanish phonics, nor was I a native speaker of the language.

I shared the classroom with their regular teacher. She was a good teacher and had high expectations.

To cope with the stress, I practiced martial arts (Tae Kwon Do and Tai Chi) four or five times a week and used Healing Breath work and Rebirthing to process my frustration and help me stay connected to my *chi* energy.

Finally I realized I was never going to succeed unless I upgraded my skills. I went to a private school in Ensenada, Mexico, and asked them to teach me Spanish phonics. That made life much easier, and I actually succeeded in teaching these kids how to read and write phonically in Spanish.

Putting the Pieces Together

I've had many opportunities to teach in kindergarten classes and introduce children to the heartfelt melodies of Scott Kalechstein.

One of my favorites, and one the children always adore, is called 'Putting the Pieces Together'. It's a cheerful song, and the children enjoy the melody and accompanying rhythmic hand movements.

The song has significance for all ages. Its words reflect our struggle to put our lives together so we can function in a viable and joyful way.

As a singer, songwriter, recording artist, speaker, minister, workshop leader and writer, Scott wears many hats. He shares his original songs internationally at conferences, workshops, churches, weddings, and private gatherings—wherever people are open to a heart centered approach to learning, growing and healing. A pioneer in the field of song portraits, Scott is known for his unique ability to create a song on the spot. In all that he does, he serves as a wise, gentle and humorous escort for those making the transition from suffering to celebration, from fear to love.

Putting the Pieces Together
Old Man Jigsaw he was one
Went to pieces just for fun
Now the time to do the puzzle has come
Putting the pieces together
(Repeated)

Humpty Dumpty fall on the floor
Putting him together was quite a chore
Now he's back and ready for more
Putting the pieces together
(Repeated)

Mother Rainbow had a dream
She saw her colors were part of a team
She told them 'You're not as separate as you seem"
Let's start putting the pieces together.
(Repeated)

From outer space the earth looks fine
There are no boundaries or country signs

Boundaries are fine but there comes a time
For putting the pieces together
(Repeated)

You have your piece I have mine
Between ourselves we drew a line
We finally found our peace of mind
By putting the pieces together
                    — Scott Kalechstein

English As A Second Language

Children are great language learners. I worked helping children with limited English proficiency improve their reading and writing. Using a variety of approaches, including gymnastics, drama, art and dance, I was able to help all thirty or forty students succeed at their individual levels.

During the summer I succeeded in teaching English as a Second Language to a group of thirty-two fifth and sixth graders. This class was tough. The kids wanted to play. It was summer, and they needed a break. Yet I was firm with them and held high expectations, and their improvement was dramatic.

Joseph Stella and The Japanese Students

Art is a wonderful form of self-expression and release of tension. I have consistently used art to help students experience a release of tension. I enjoy using the eclectic art of Joseph Stella as a model. He was an Italian American immigrant. His eclectic works included abstracts of the Brooklyn Bridge, and Coney Island in Brooklyn, New York, renditions of flowers, plants from the Caribbean, working class blue collar laborers at steel mills in Pittsburgh, Pennsylvania, profiles of individuals, and graceful white swans.

I shared his prolific works of art with a group of English As A Second Language students from a Japanese University and a group of second grade children at a local school in San Diego, California. I asked the Japanese students to create their own masterpieces. The Japanese were shy and reluctant to speak and the art project helped to reduce their tension. It became easier for them to express themselves in English and describe their completed works of art. Their artwork included renditions of Japanese cartoon characters, floral arrangements, animals, and geishas. The children created beautiful reflections of flowers and animals in their artwork. Art does help individuals to express themselves in a creative non-threatening way. It helps people to release tension and relax. Art Therapy has become an important integrative alternative method for helping people to connect with their inner child and to express their adult frustrations. It creates a sense of safety and helps to release the external layers of emotion to begin to access deeper feelings of distress. This is a wonderful activity especially for seniors experiencing isolation and loneliness.

Self-Esteem for Third Graders

Children often need help to feel better about themselves.

I recently completed a long term substituting contract helping insecure kids raise their self-esteem. Some of these kids had very negative attitudes about themselves and their ability to learn. Using positive affirmations, spoken with conviction and accompanied by congruent body language, I helped them raised their self-image enough to enjoy success in the classroom.

Raising self-esteem in the classroom is not easily accomplished; it requires vast amounts of patience, self-discipline, firmness, and an understanding of the nature of distress. A teacher who has successfully worked through his or her own issues and is passionate about the process can achieve miracles by combining affirmations with physical exercise (stretching and cardio-vascular activities).

The most important ingredient of all is establishing self and empathetic love.

Creative Counseling

George was on the verge of tears. His eyes and facial expression revealed the pain he was experiencing.

I was substituting at a school for a counselor when a teacher brought this eight-year-old into the office. He was having difficulty concentrating on his studies, she told me. His parents were splitting up. George was in distress, nervous and distraught.

I sensed that he felt guilty about his parents' separation. I spoke softly to him, telling him it was not his responsibility, that he was never to think in those terms. He relaxed and began to let go, and his tears flowed in an ever-increasing stream.

He seemed to have a great need to express his feelings to someone who could empathize and be responsible for him. I whispered in his ear again and again that he was not to blame for his parents' splitting up. I suggested he was doing the best he could under the circumstances and that he should be proud of himself.

This boy somehow was able to hear me. I continued to give him loving support and asked him to write positive affirmations about himself in a notebook. I instructed the teacher to send George to the regular counselor for follow-up.

Points To Ponder

Few are those who don't experience some kind of health challenges as a result of the stresses of today's world. Migraine headache is a very common complaint. Consider the following:

* If you find yourself in a stressful situation with children, how are you going to help them if you are sacrificing yourself? What can you do to take care of your own physical, emotional and mental health?

Thirteen

Surviving the Job Jungle

Temporary teaching jobs don't provide much financial security, and I have often sought other ways to stabilize my income. The uncertainty of my job situation has been a constant source of tension for me. Processing my feelings about it has often felt like the release of an addiction, bringing on an experience of concurrent warmth and icy chills.

My blood pressure had increased to 170/100.

"Inordinately high," the doctor told me. "I want you to monitor your pressure for the next month."

I knew my high blood pressure was a direct result of my fear of being out of a job. As I grew older, I'd become uncomfortably aware of age discrimination in the job market. Intense releases in Rebirthing sessions took my blood pressure back down to 118/69. As I began to worry about job availability again, it would go back up, and come back down again, as I'd do the work to release the strain. The correlation was too obvious to doubt.

I also found certain nutritional supplements helpful in bringing my blood pressure down: a high potency mega-B complex, vitamin C, St. Johns Wort, Kava Kava, and Inositol with lecithin, and garlic. I eliminated refined carbohydrates, starch and sugars, and began eating more vegetables, cabbage, broccoli, brussels sprouts, salmon and mackerel.

Only I can change my life.
No one can do it for me.
        —Carol Burnett

To HMO and Back

One time when I found myself in need of a job I applied for a position as an admitting representative for a major Health Maintenance Organization. With my background in human services, it seemed a 'natural'.

Getting the job was a job in itself. I had to make over forty phone calls to get the initial appointment, sit through exam after exam, and subject myself to three intense in-depth interviews. It was a grueling experience.

Finally I was hired. My job was to record the data on individual patients to determine their level of financial responsibility.

During the initial training period I began to get some idea of the absurdity of the system I would be working in. I really began to wonder about this HMO when one of my supervisors told me he had quit and returned to work seven times! The amount of information I had to learn to do my job well was overwhelming. Just keeping up with the changes was a daunting task.

The training schedule rotated every few days. Initially I worked from five forty-five in the morning to two in the afternoon. After a few days I was switched to the opposite schedule, coming in at five forty-five in the evening and working until two in the morning. On the next shift I came in at ten-thirty at night and worked until seven in the morning, and a few days later the schedule switched me to coming in at seven in the morning and leaving at three-thirty in the afternoon. On top of all that, I worked different days every week. Needless to say, it was not a 'gig' for the inflexible individual!

I was happy to have an opportunity to work, however, so I was careful to do everything right as rain. I always arrived on time, I was diligent in performing my duties, and I was always respectful to others. I worked very hard to make each adjustment to the constantly evolving work scenarios.

The pressure was intense. To handle the stress and preserve my sanity, I engaged in Healing Breath sessions, Primal Scream therapy, prayer, kinesiology chiropractic, Peer Co-Counseling, metaphysical counseling and Tae Kwon Do.

I thought I was doing a great job. I had learned my duties and responsibilities better than most, and was impressed with my own performance. Ultimately however, I would never be good enough to satisfy my employer, who claimed I was too slow in learning the job.

At the end of my first month on the job I was laid-off. Laid-off! I was devastated, but I continued to counsel faithfully. The resultant personal growth was enormous. I accumulated greater strength and maturity as a result of this trying experience.

Growth experiences like this one are always tough, but I had discovered I could always choose to grow regardless of the hardships I encounter. The experience led me to a startling conclusion, long since confirmed by a multitude of similar experiences: *I am my own salvation, role model, and hero.*

Bank Officer Training in San Jose

Another time, training as a bank officer for a bank in San Diego, I was sent to a program in San Jose.

We were twenty trainees from different areas of the state, mostly from the San Francisco Bay area. What a fascinating collage of cultural backgrounds! The training included a demonstration of social class differences. Ten of us were asked to address the question of our experience growing up in our particular social class. Each person described a vastly different set of circumstances that had framed their personality. It was a fascinating insight into social class differences in the good ol' U.S.A.

The training was challenging for me. I made the adjustment by practicing meditation, yoga, Tae Kwon Do and breath work to calm my anxiety, and successfully completed the course.

One day as I was finishing a Tae Kwon Do and meditation session on a grass mat across from the San Jose Hilton, I was approached by a man of Hispanic descent who introduced himself as Jorge. His manner was anxious and hesitant.

"Could you please tell me how I could learn to meditate and exercise? I need to reduce my fearfulness," he said in Spanish.

Jorge told me he was unemployed and in therapy at a local outpatient center. He said his medication was not helping him, and he was having difficulty sleeping. I had compassion for his troubles and was happy to give him a demonstration of Healing Breath Work on the grass mat. He appeared enthusiastic about the process and seemed to understand the significance of releasing the toxic energy.

I finished the two-week intensive bank training and returned to San Diego.

As I began to adjust to my new position as a bank officer, I felt like I was being reborn. My whole being vibrated with excitement and enthusiasm as I expressed new intentions of expanding to meet new challenges.

I also felt the old anxieties from my birth trauma rising from the ashes. I used my breath work to become my own salvation once again. I felt myself expanding emotionally as I adjusted to my new duties and responsibilities with each breath session.

I was and am my own salvation, but I was not alone. I could feel God's love with me as I used the circular breath to release my fears. The good Lord was clearly helping me to find more of my own wholeness.

Learning Tae Kwon Do and Tai Chi Chih, participating in Iyengar and Vini Yoga, and continuing with Peer Co-Counseling and Primal Therapy helped me become effective, relaxed, and confident in my employment. I also connected with San Diego's 'New Age' community, found a group of Sufi dancers, and made the acquaintance of breath workers and Rebirthers at Saddahna fellowship.

Healing Practice: Kinesiology Chiropractic

Kinesiology Chiropractic is a wonderful form of readjusting the balance of the body. The chiropractor performs muscle testing to determine muscle strength. Adjustments are made to bones, vertebrae, and joints accordingly. The goal is to return the body to alignment. I've tried several practitioners and have found gentle healers to be preferable.

Healing Practice: Iyengar Yoga

Iyengar Yoga offers a precise methodology that integrates alignment, balance, strength and flexibility. Its focus is on posture and form. I have experienced this form of yoga in San Diego on a consistent basis, and have always felt considerably better after a good stretching and centering session.

At one point I had developed osteoarthritis as a result of the removal of a torn lateral meniscus in my right knee. This type of yoga helped me to manage the condition.

Healing Practice: Vini Yoga

Vini Yoga has a focus on function, posture, and breath. This form of yoga is excellent as it can be used for both relaxation and to access profounder emotional release through Breath Work and Rebirthing.

Healing Practice: T'ai Chi Chih

I came into intimate knowledge of T'ai Chi Chih, a unique martial art derivative, at a Whole Being Weekend held in Julian, California. Justin Stone, a Master of the ancient Chinese martial art, created this unique style in 1974.

T'ai Chi, which dates back approximately two thousand years, has many styles. It was created to allow people to tap into and actively circulate the 'Life Force' that the ancient Chinese called *chi*, thus promoting greater health, serenity, joy and well being. The style of T'ai Chi familiar to us in the United States is a slow, non-aggressive form of meditation, the philosophical opposite of the aggressiveness of Tae Kwon Do.

T'ai Chi Chih can be practiced by people of all ages, including those impacted by a variety of physical and emotional challenges. I don't know of another personal growth activity that creates as powerful and subtle a holistic connection with our life force.

The breath is our connection with our life force energy, and is a significant element for connecting with and releasing stress from the body in conjunction with the T'ai Chi Chih movements.

Susan D. Patterson is presently a teacher of T'ai Chi Chih in San Diego. When I asked her to comment about the efficacy of this modality, she wrote the following:

"T'ai Chi Chih (TCC) is a gentle movement meditation that I have practiced for 17 years. When I first started practicing I had severe stomach problems and chronic lower back pain. I was told after many medical tests that there was not a diagnosis for either and that I would probably have to be on pain medication for the rest of my life. Within two weeks of learning a few moves of TCC the stomach pains went away, and within a year the back pain was gone also. TCC is a part of my everyday routine now and I continue to be in optimum health. The 'silent time' during my practice is very special and spills over into my everyday life, allowing for calmness even during some of the most hectic situations. I wish there were a way to add this to everyone's day so that we could have a more peaceful, relaxed, and healthy society."

The Medical Center at the University of California at San Diego has conducted two controlled studies in the past three years on the effects of TCC on chronic lower back pain and the immune system. Their researchers documented that TCC significantly reduces lower back pain and dramatically enhances the immune system.

Healing Practice: Nutritional Supplements

The use of certain nutritional supplements has helped immensely in my healing on all levels. I've used Echinacea as a natural anti-biotic when I've experienced viral infections.

Points To Ponder

Personal growth activities helped me tremendously in adjusting to new employment opportunities. Consider:

- Are you in a job that doesn't suit you? What could you gain by using a variety of personal growth activities to deal with it?
- How can you use your experiences on the job as opportunities to find your authentic purpose, your true mission in life?
- If you run a business, how can you integrate personal growth methodologies to create happier, healthier, more productive employees?

Fourteen

San Diego Stories

Of the many experiences I've had in San Diego that have shown me the value of my own personal growth, the following three stand out in my mind as worthy of reporting.

A Phone Call From Sasha

"Are you the author of 'I Dare to Heal'? Are you Joel Vorensky?"

"Yes, I am. Yes, I wrote it."

"Hi. My name is Sasha. I picked up your flyer for your book at devotional singing the other night. Joel, I'm desperate. Please, I need your help!"

I asked her what the problem was.

"My life is in complete turmoil," she responded. "I don't know what to do anymore. I want to end it! My boyfriend left, he took everything, and now I have nothing to live for! You know me, Joel, I'm not usually like this. I'm never like this. I need help."

"I know you? Have we met?"

"I sat behind you at Religious Science Church, remember? And I go to devotional singing. You know me—always joyful, dancing, outgoing. Remember me? Sasha!"

Yes, I remembered Sasha. I remembered her as a woman who seemed joyful but carried a heavy burden; a vibration that I intuitively knew was self-destructive. I remembered her anxious expression, her insecure body language. A lost soul, a soul searching for some stability and anchoring in the world!

I comforted her. I couldn't help but have compassion for her. She told me how difficult it had been for her to call me.

"It's OK to reach out, Sasha. It's OK to reach out to me. I want you to know you're fine, " I said. "It's OK."

"You mean it's OK for me to ask for help?"

"Yes, Sasha, it is perfectly OK for you to reach out and ask for help. People love it when you do that!"

She protested.

"I love you for reaching out, Sasha. And if someone can't be there for you, don't take it as a rejection of you. It's not about you; it's about them! I want you to know that! It just means they're not available to you. It means nothing about you! Please have that awareness." I repeated this again and again, until Sasha was able to hear it and accept it.

"But my boyfriend left me! I've lost my car, my inheritance, and my house! Everything is gone! I have nothing left in my life!" I could hear that she was about ready to break down in tears.

"It doesn't matter, Sasha, you are loved! You are loved for Sasha herself! Please remember that; know that, dear heart. Know that you are loved!" I repeated this sentence in a warm, tender, caring tone of voice. She seemed somewhat comforted.

Sasha told me someone was helping her find a place to live, and an acquaintance was taking care of her dental work. She claimed to have an interest in learning a skill. She said she had no money and wasn't sure how she would go about learning a trade.

"Opportunities do exist, Sasha," I encouraged. "Just take small steps in obtaining the skills necessary to become successful."

"I guess small steps could turn out to be important ones," she observed.

I agreed. "Choose life," I said. "Make that choice of life from moment to moment, knowing that you are loved. Miracles do happen! They will happen to you in your life as well."

Sasha liked the sound of my voice and appreciated my encouragement. She sounded much happier by the time I said good-bye to her.

Jake And Judy

The Religious Science sermon had ended.

I figured I could use some support, so I moved to the back corner of the room where the spiritual practitioners were waiting to help anyone who needed a prayer treatment.

"Joel?"

It was Jake, with his wife, Judy. We had met several times at the church. Judy was an intense woman in her early twenties, with body language reflective of some inner stress and an alarming quickness to her manner of speech. She had a history of physical illness and severe emotional anxiety. I could see she was on the verge of hysterics, and Jake seemed helpless to comfort her.

"Joel, I think we need your help. Judy—"

I was looking for help myself that day. How could I possibly be of any help to anyone else? I was at a loss for words. Then my eyes caught Judy's needy glance. Oh well, time to put my own fears aside. My twenty-eight years of training as a Peer Co-Counselor came in handy in situations like this. I took a deep breath to stabilize myself so I could be there for her in her distress. Touching her hands and maintaining an authentic empathetic attitude, I spoke to her in an attentive, supportive, low-keyed tone.

Within a few minutes Dorothy, a Religious Science practitioner, made her way over to us. She sat with us and helped in supporting Judy.

Judy told us she was upset because she'd recently been diagnosed with cancer. She flirted with hysteria as Dorothy and I gave her loving support. She was sure the cancer had been visited on her because of something she'd done wrong.

"It's God's punishment, because I had sinned against him," she kept saying. Dorothy and I assured her in a firm and caring way that it was not. We encouraged her to make use of a variety of supportive resources to alleviate her negative and fearful thought patterns: prayer, Healing Breath, Rebirthing, positive affirmations, meditation, and a pro-active life-style.

A physician who does counseling with cancer patients has advised me that eighty percent of disease is the result of accumulated physical and emotional distress. It is my belief that consistent and effective Rebirthing practice can help to cleanse distress on a cellular level and bring about the emotional level of healing necessary to combat a disease like cancer.

We passed this practical advice along to Judy, hoping it would help her to take charge of her life, and advised her to seek additional support in the future.

A Test of Trust

The revisions of the chapters were going so well! I had paid Max to do the initial edit, and I was pleased with his work.

Then one day I couldn't find him. He'd disappeared! What had happened to him? My e-mails went unanswered. His telephone was disconnected. I sent him a letter via 'snail mail' and received no reply.

My anxiety level went through the roof. This was the first book I'd ever written. I was vulnerable. I thought I'd found an editor I could trust, and then the bottom dropped out.

No! This couldn't be! I refused to let go of my faith.

Max was a good man, a spiritual man. I'd heard him speak of his connection to Spirit in wonderful expressive tones to his beloved Samantha, who would sit quietly and listen with a glow in her heart. Such a lovely couple! They seemed to complement each other so well. I knew all relationships had issues and challenges, but it was beautiful to observe the loving connection between these two individuals whose lives seemed to melt into harmony and blissful oneness. The more I thought about Max and Samantha, the more I knew there had to be some extenuating circumstance.

But I couldn't still the voice of worry.

San Diego has an unfortunate history as a 'scam city'. Perhaps Max had swindled me? Left town with my money? The thought didn't make sense—he was so enthusiastic about my manuscript! There must have been some other reason for his disappearance. I mailed him a registered letter, 'return receipt required'.

Perhaps the print shop administrator who had referred Max to me in the first place might know what had happened to him. I phoned the printer, who informed me that the administrator had been terminated. My anxiety skyrocketed.

Once again my personal growth modalities were proving to be a valuable resource. Two breath sessions, a Tae Kwon Do session, Peer Co-Counseling and prayer calmed me down, and I held onto my faith.

The breath sessions were particularly helpful because they helped me release my victim feelings. I arrived at what was for me a meaningful distinction. I may have been victimized, but I was not a victim!

And maybe, just maybe, Max hadn't decided to rip me off. Maybe there was some other explanation. I decided to give the whole matter over to the good Lord.

Upon arriving home after teaching school I listened to my message recorder. Max's voice came over the machine, explaining that his phone and e-mail line had been disconnected and that he had had to leave town temporarily because of the unexpected illness of a family member.

When we finally got together in person I listened to Max attentively and responded by telling him of my fears and my faith. He recognized that I had been rightfully upset, and apologized.

I was glad I had refused to give in to the voice of doubt. Intuitively I'd known Max was a good man, and my intuition had served me well. Our ability to listen and respond to each other in a rational way allowed us to regroup easily and move ahead with our collaboration.

Fifteen

Spiritual Connection
and Synchronicity

Like many people, I have experienced wondrous events for which I have no explanation. When this happens to me, I smile and thank God I've noticed! Such events invariably impact me in a positive way and encourage my faith.

Paging Joel...

In a Jewish singles group not long ago the Rabbi asked us how we connected with our Jewish roots. He insisted on the importance of that connection, and his point was well taken.

When my turn came to respond, I said: "We connect with our Jewish roots through a mutual opening of our hearts and expressions of love for one another." Others suggested they would connect with their Jewish beliefs and nature by mentally and physically holding onto their religious traditions.

We came to agree that true connection with our Jewish roots required both the heart and the intellect. I shared that I had discovered that the encouragement I had received from both Jewish people and non-Jews supportive of the Jewish way of life had strengthened my appreciation for my Jewish heritage.

Five minutes later my pager began to vibrate, signaling me that somebody wanted to get hold of me right away. What I saw on my pager screen was nothing less than amazing! It was showing the name 'Jesus'!

I simply could not believe my eyes. I stared at it in awe for a few seconds, then asked a friend sitting close to me to read the message and tell me what she saw. She was shocked to see that it read 'Jesus'. She took the pager and asked a friend sitting on the other side of her to read the display.

"It's saying the time is 7:54 p.m.," she said.

My friend was incredulous. She checked the screen again; it was still displaying the name 'Jesus'. Handing the pager back to me, she whispered in my ear: "Is she is so narrow minded she can't see what it says?"

Perhaps the message had been just for the two of us. We both saw Jesus as an ally. The lesson was clear: an openness to others, not just to those similar to ourselves, is essential for us to connect with the roots of who we really are.

This was an unexplainable but spiritually connecting experience for both of us, what I would call an outstanding spiritual encounter.

The Old Turtle

One particular experience filling in as a substitute teacher for a sixth grade class had turned out to be a tough assignment. I'd tried nearly everything in my bag of tricks. Finally, at my wits' end, I went to the bookshelf. My hand was drawn to Wood's book, *The Old Turtle* (Cheng-Khee Chee, 1992). I'd never read it. I took it out and opened it and began to read aloud.

An enormous silence descended on the room as the attention of the thirty-five sixth graders became riveted on this metaphor about creation and God as reflective of all things. The children loved the old turtle and the story's spiritual message. They didn't even complain when I asked them to write a summary of the book.

Turning to the east in prayer (a tradition shared by Jews and Buddhists) at a Jewish Renewal Service that very same week, I found myself looking out the window at a lovely meditative garden. I was astonished to see a stone statue of the old turtle!

The Synchronicity of Numbers

My friend Tom and I had decided to meet at the singles gathering sponsored by a local newspaper at a local hotel.

I arrived at just past six. The hosts were distributing random door prize numbers. My number was 69964.

Twenty or thirty minutes went by, and perhaps fifty or more people entered the hotel. Each one was issued a number. Tom and I walked outside onto the patio, where there was a buffet dinner and a beautiful view of the bay.

A young woman with a lovely smile approached, and we began a casual conversation. Linda seemed open and friendly. She was a tall, thin, and quite attractive. Her brown hair and dark eyes were highlighted by a lovely smile. We became acquainted and spoke of our common interest in metaphysics. We felt a pleasant energetic connection, and Tom seemed to enjoy the conversation as well. It just seemed as though we were all three meant to connect! A genuine rapport was developing, and we spoke about keeping in touch with each other.

There must have been several hundred participants in the hotel by the time we returned to the main hall. The master of ceremonies began to call out the door prize numbers. Tom, Linda, and I had all come in at different times, but we were surprised to find that our numbers were consecutive—Tom's was 69962, Linda's was 69963, and mine was 69964. We had already remarked on the similarities of our astrological charts. We looked at each other in astonishment and disbelief. Mere coincidence? Hmmmm....

'Angelnicity'

I began a temporary position in the business office of a local hospital, where I was temporarily assigned to a computer in a partitioned cubicle. A porcelain angel sat on top of the computer with a wreath around its head.

Three days later I was transferred to another computer terminal. There, seated on top of it, was a similar angel!

No other computer in the Business Services office had its own resident angel.

How perfect.

The Dolphin Connection

DOLPHIN...
Breathe with me
Breath of the Divine
Manna (life force) of the Universe
In oneness we entwine.

At a Sacred Ceremonial Sweat Lodge I attended, we were asked to select from a deck of animal cards prior to entering the sacred lodge *(inipi)*. Without any real understanding of its significance, I selected the card of Dolphin.

When I revisited the Sweat Lodge the following month I decided not to select another animal card. Intuitively I knew the dolphin was appropriate to my spirit. The dolphin is playful, trusting, loving, and enjoys its freedom in the sea. Symbolically, it is a messenger—messenger of Spirit! I have often watched the dolphins surf the waves off the San Diego coast and have long been in awe of their life force.

There is a book known as *Medicine Cards, The Discovery of Power through the Ways of Animals.* I had never opened this book to read about any animal. There must be thirty or forty different animals featured in the book. I was curious about the dolphin and decided to investigate the significance of this mammal. I astonished myself by opening the book to the page on Dolphin without even looking in the table of contents. I was further astonished to read the poem (above). Seeing it in the light of what I had learned about Dolphin as spiritual messenger, I realized Dolphin connects with Spirit by way of the breath.

How appropriate for me!

God's Knee

My right knee had bothered me since I'd injured it as a young boy by falling on a stick. The resulting infection had caused deterioration of the cartilage. The pain wasn't limited to the knee—my lower back hurt all the time, and I had migraine headaches and shooting reflex pain in my shoulder, arm, elbow, and hand.

The injury hadn't been without its bright side. In the '60s, when I was about to be drafted into the Army, the military doctors ignored all the problems I presented them until they found the records of a surgery I'd had to have some of the cartilage removed from my knee at the age of eighteen. When they found those records, they offered me a deferment. Perhaps it was divine intervention at a young age that kept me from being sent to Southeast Asia!

It was springtime, years later. The pain in my knee had recently escalated. I was having difficulty sleeping. Standing, walking and braking my automobile had become painful activities, and I had started to limp. The signs of a major problem were evident.

I visited a local health clinic. Doctor Buenviaje claimed my knee merited evaluation by an orthopedic physician and sent me for x-rays. The resulting diagnosis was severe osteoarthritis. Doctor Byron 'Butch' Butler, head of the Department of Orthopedics and a specialist in knee replacements, claimed God's-given knee could never be successfully replaced. But I knew better!

The problem was that I had no medical insurance. How was I going to pay for knee surgery?

I had been employed by a local hospital on an on-call basis. Perhaps I could obtain employment once again through them and then apply for the insurance? I spoke with Angelica D'Angeles. The personnel assistant, who told me there could be a job for me if I had been employed by the hospital during the past year. I told her I had worked in neonatology, but that it had been over a year.

Angelica was an Angel! She found me a temporary job in spite of the time lapse, and I purchased the medical insurance through the hospital.

I believe Angelica was an angel sent by 'Great Spirit'. She was reassigned to another division two weeks after I started my job. I never did see her again or obtained subsequent opportunities of employment at the hospital.

I received a total knee joint replacement at Chanukah. This was Gods gift to me. This *was* 'God's Knee'.

Points To Ponder

All too often humans have no control over circumstances and situations. I learned to have more faith in spirituality through the above examples! Consider the following:

- What unexplained experiences have you had that could empower your connection with Spirit and with your Self?
- What have you learned from the unexplained connections between spontaneous events?
- Why are these events important to your spiritual growth?
- Do you think you could strengthen your own or others' faith in self, other people and Spirit by sharing your metaphysical experiences with them?

Sixteen

The Seam Between Heaven and Hell

Pain is a more terrible lord of mankind than death itself.

Dr. Albert Sweitzer

My knee had been causing me a lot of trouble. I knew I needed to have it replaced. Having talked to a number of people who had undergone total knee replacement surgery, I knew it was likely to be a painful ordeal. But the sleepless nights were escalating, and the pain had begun to impact my ability to concentrate at work.

My kinesiologist chiropractor had been following the escalation of my pain, and encouraged me to have a total knee joint replacement. I was surprised at his encouragement, since he was known for his conservative approach in advising patients regarding major surgery. He said he'd done everything he could to sustain me over the last two years, and now it was time for me to bite the bullet and undergo the procedure. We did a visualization and a celebrated a positive outcome to this surgery.

I voiced my concerns to the assistant surgeon prior to the surgery.

"There's typically a lot of pain in this type of an operation," he told me. "It might help to have analgesic medicine pumped into the joint. I know of someone doing research on a pump that might alleviate the intensity of the pain, if you're interested."

Of course I was interested. I agreed to try it.

The surgical procedure was scheduled for early Tuesday morning. Anxious to be done with the suffering from this old injury, I looked forward to a new freedom. A friend accompanied me to the hospital for emotional support.

I awoke from the surgery in a private room, my right knee bandaged and in a great deal of discomfort. The pain continued. It was excruciating, and the nurse spoke with the physicians about it. They prescribed morphine in addition to the analgesics administered by the pump.

The morphine shots gave me a rest from my discomfort, but sleep was still out of reach. The nurse said she wasn't surprised, and added that the pump had not provided relief to the other patients who'd used it, either.

I requested the pump be removed.

"But you really haven't given it a fair trial," the assistant surgeon objected. "I have confidence that the administration of the analgesic in pulsating rhythms will prove beneficial."

"This pump is going to help you, I know it can," the researcher chimed in. It was obvious she had some personal stake in the success of the pump. "What would you say is the level of your discomfort, on a scale of one to ten?"

"Ten!" It infuriated me that she seemed more interested in the success of the pump than in the alleviation of my pain.

"The pump has exactly what you need for your pain," she insisted. "If you'll just calm down, I'm sure you'll realize it's helping."

"I have been calm," I said, not very calmly. "The only thing that's upsetting me is your cavalier attitude. You are not the one experiencing the pain. Even with the morphine, it's excruciating!" The nerve of this woman! To try to sell me on the benefits of a pump while I was in this vulnerable condition?

The nurse told me it would take twenty-four to thirty-six hours before the pump could administer enough medicine to make a difference.

"Is that right?"

"It could take that long," the assisting surgeon admitted.

"Why didn't you advise me of this?" I raged. "Isn't this significant information? Get this thing out of here, now! And close the door and leave me alone!"

The pump was removed, and the door was shut. I was glad they'd given me a private room. I knew what I had to do, and I didn't want to be disturbed.

I began the Rebirthing breath.

Relief was immediate. I felt momentary peace and rest after every profound release. The Rebirthing circular breath was a savior!

I cut through any resistance to connecting with the pain by pulling air in through my mouth and filling my belly with it, as deeply as possible. I was tenacious!

The knee pain was tenacious as well. Relief came—and left—with each breath.

Now I felt alone in my private room, abandoned, isolated. Were these feelings just restimulation of my birth experience? I could feel paranoia taking over. Feelings of helpless and anxiety engulfed me.

I accessed these feelings by pulling air in through my mouth once again. My terror kept the air from flowing smoothly into my abdominal cavity, but I was determined.

I pushed through the resistance and felt the air flow into the abdominal cavity and down into my pelvis! I held my breath, then let it go with a scream, a primal scream. The pain surged out of me in volcanic proportions. I released the feelings of terror again, and again, and again, until peace filled my body and my mind was at rest. In the process I connected with an incredible, all-pervasive light! Going beyond the limits of suffering, I became one with Spirit!

I slipped into meditation, a sure way to relax and mellow out. My blood pressure returned to normal. Afterward the nurses told me they couldn't believe how relaxed I became, when just forty minutes before I'd been so anxious. They were bewildered.

"Well, it wasn't magic," I told them. "The primal breathing and meditation took self-discipline and tenacity on my part."

I continued my Rebirthing practice, listening to tapes of spiritual music that helped to keep me calm. My anxiety released, I was able to stay clear in my mind and carry on rational conversations with the hospital personnel. I stated my needs clearly, and told them of my intuitive reactions to the drugs. My ability to maintain clarity of mind and stay connected to my conviction and my will was significant in helping me communicate effectively.

I began physical therapy to rehabilitate my knee, using the power of the breath. They released me from the hospital and transferred me to a skilled nursing care facility to continue my physical therapy.

I felt very fortunate to be assigned to the best skilled nursing care center in San Diego County, with the ultimate staff: a visiting physician, a treatment and charge nurse, nursing aids, and physical therapists. I could rest in the rose garden, eat gourmet food, and 'enjoy' all the benefits of modern physical therapy rooms—all this in an uplifting environment.

My leg was still swollen to twice its normal size, as big as a watermelon, and even an ice pack didn't help. The resident physician suspected complications. He ordered a Doppler Echocardiography, also known as an ultrasound test.

"We just want to be sure there's no blood clot," he explained.

I had been treated with blood thinners to prevent clots. If a clot developed in my leg and traveled to my heart, lung, or brain, a major health problem could result. I'd been anxious about the swelling, but now the potential of a blood clot really worried me. I used the Healing Breath to calm myself.

The ultrasound results were negative, yet the swelling and pain continued, with no apparent healing. Not satisfied, the physician ordered another ultrasound.

Aha! A blood clot had appeared, below the knee. The doctor administered additional blood thinner.

"The additional blood thinner will make you vulnerable to bleeding," he told me. "Nothing to worry about, but we'll keep our eye on you." Nothing to worry about? Obviously he didn't know me very well.

He also suspected an infection, and ordered the antibiotic Keflex, to which I reacted with red rashes and blotches from my torso to my feet. I asked the nurse to discontinue the Keflex.

For several nights I struggled through a cycle of pain from the swelling, fever, and night sweats. The surgical specialist told me it was important to acquire a range of motion in the knee joint to prevent scarring. He suggested I switch the focus of my attention from the pain and swelling to increasing my range of motion.

Easier said than done. The pain from the swelling was excruciating. The quad muscles in my right thigh had been atrophying for years. This, combined with the trauma of the surgery, was causing muscle constrictions in my right leg. I would have to work extra hard and negotiate with my pain to break through the constrictions. I knew I had an arduous job ahead of me.

The breath work offered me immediate access to the huge pain I was experiencing, allowing me to release it. How fortunate I was to have skilled counselors to help me through the release! One practitioner assisted with me at my bedside through a profound and moving emotional release. I was tenacious and continued breathing and accessing God's Light. Another professional applied Healing Touch on my knee, which also helped.

At 2:30 one morning I was in terrible pain and turned to a telephone crisis counselor for help. I set up a table with candy, cards, plants, balloons and party hats to inspire me. I watched cartoons and comedy on video. *Laughter* was truly my best medicine.

Did you catch that statement? The ability to engage and release yourself using your sense of humor is so significant it often goes unnoticed. There is a lightness of being, a sense of proportion that flows from a well-developed and engaged sense of humor. Life is at times very serious indeed; troubles abound, but no matter what, humor informs us that all is not lost, that 'this too will pass'. Laughter brought me immediately into the presence of the NOW!

I received loving support from many friends by phone and through personal visits, along with phone calls and visits from ministers and rabbis. I ate well and focused my attention on helping others. I even started leading prayers with other patients, which I found quite beneficial.

I used my feelings as a catalyst to strengthen myself, to heal, to create more love within myself. When friends and family couldn't contact me, I accessed and released my disappointment and any negative thoughts I had harbored about them. I sent my friends light and love.

I had finished most of this book before my surgery, and had mailed off a hard copy of the manuscript with a check to my editor the day before I went into the hospital. She called me on my last day at the hospital to tell me it hadn't arrived. She said she'd called the post office and they'd said that because I'd sent it 'book rate' over the Christmas holidays it could take up to fourteen days to reach her.

On the fifteenth day she called me at the nursing home.

"It still hasn't come," she said.

"Well then, come on over to the nursing home and I'll write you a check. I'll have my friend Mark check my mailbox and see if the manuscript has come back, and he can get it to you. If it hasn't come back, we'll have to figure out something else."

She arrived at the nursing home just before lunch, and I wrote her a check. When she asked after my condition I told her about the pain and the complications, and the breath work that I'd been doing to pull myself through the experience. We finished our business and I walked her to the elevator.

"But you're walking. That's good. And you're still smiling!"

"Well, I've been doing a lot of work on myself."

She gave me a warm hug and stepped into the elevator, then turned and stepped out again.

"I just want to say one thing," she said. "You are amazing! You are an inspiration. You are really living what you're writing about. Joel Vorensky, I love you!"

This woman hardly knew me, in fact we'd only met once in person, a year before. I can still hear her words of appreciation for my ability to hold peace in my heart through this time of extreme difficulty. (The manuscript had been returned to me by the post office, it turned out, and was there when my friend Stan went to check).

Then came the most exciting surprise of all: my daughter phoned from Scandinavia, something she'd seldom done over the years. I had been praying to receive a call from her. This was the most exhilarating and uplifting emotional experience of the whole episode! I would go through this whole experience all over again just to feel the exhilaration of hearing her voice over the phone.

God willing, I won't have to.

Points To Ponder

Personal growth activities such as Rebirthing, Primal Therapy Healing Touch, Peer Co-Counseling, prayer, listening to music, along with taking nutritional supplements, helped me master post surgical acute chronic pain with complications. Consider:

- If you have chronic excruciating pain or know someone who does, could some of these modalities be helpful in reducing the pain and maintaining a positive quality of life?

Free At Last: My Right of Passage

For twenty-eight years I had been on a journey to find myself, to discover my true nature, to move from a state of high anxiety to a state of emotional security.

Over the weekend of May 3rd, 1998, I took a Sadhana workshop and a Breath Work session at the Life Institute of San Diego County. That weekend I made my transition into spiritual wholeness.

As always, the release of deep-seated, helpless terror came as I moved into the experience of confinement in my mother's womb.

I released the terror again and again, for what seemed an eternity. Once I began feeling and releasing my so-called pain, I noticed that the feelings had become painless. They were just old feelings that needed to come out of me, nothing more. I realized then that the common belief that feelings are painful is a learned cultural message that has no validity.

At that point I started to become healthier, younger, more aware, happier. I actually felt an emotional shift-taking place as I left behind my old insecurity. Moving through the layers of distress by way of the breath, feeling the sensations of infant Joel became a totally fascinating experience.

As each wave of release washed over me, I found myself in the womb again, changing my emotional experience from terror to security. I felt a sense of space opening up within my consciousness and a growing connection with what I would call 'self'.

I was evolving into a new, stronger, more self-confident me. With each release of breath the emotional space became larger, able to hold greater feelings of well-being, joy and zest for life.

I felt like celebrating. I was truly *alive!*

For the first time in twenty-eight years, I knew the freedom that comes only with emotional security, the joy of knowing I had arrived at wholeness.

The road to wholeness hadn't been an easy one. Year after year I had had to reach inside myself to find the strength to confront my terror, grief and anger. Although I had always trusted I would find and create a healthy self, still the experience had required a great deal of persistence, patience and hard work. I had *earned* my right of passage.

The reward of personal wholeness was worth it all.

There are many who will try to discourage you from undertaking the journey to that place of darkness within yourself. "Don't go there!" they will admonish. Perhaps they are correct. Or perhaps they are just afraid, or unaware, or in need of a mentor to guide their way. Whatever they say, the choice is yours. I chose to free myself, and I have never been happier than I am right now. I encourage you to free yourself, and to love powerfully!

Life has worked out well for me. By coming to know myself so much better I've gained peace of mind and a stronger connection to Spirit. I now enjoy a greater sense of freedom in my life.

My experience is not unlike that of thousands of others who have dared to persevere in the work of freeing themselves from the traumas of the past. I have dared to heal! Can it help you to make use of one or more of the personal growth technologies available today? I encourage you to experiment for yourself, and find out. What have you got to lose, other than your trauma, low self-esteem, and self-defeating behaviors?

Workshops, Retreats, and Spiritual Groups

Much of my personal growth has come through life experience, as related in the previous chapters. This book wouldn't be complete without an excursion, however brief, into the world of self-development workshops, retreats and spiritual communities from which I have learned many of the tools that have helped me through my life experiences.

In the next eight chapters I provide accounts of my experiences in the hope they will inspire you to seek out teachers in your area who can help you on your path.

Eighteen

Three Weekend Workshops

Whole Being Weekends

Whole Being Weekends are held regularly in the mountains of San Diego County and in Idyllwild, California. Similar gatherings are offered in locales around the country; I strongly suggest you check around to find one that suits you.

Whole Being Weekends began twenty-nine years ago as sensitivity group weekends sponsored by the YMCA at San Diego State University. Bringing together spiritual healers from different backgrounds and interests, these unique weekends offer a wide variety of metaphysical activities. My favorites have included workshops in T'ai Chi Chih, Rebirthing, Sufi Dancing, Tantra (with non-sexual touching), Devotional Singing, Aware Body Massage, and Happiness Sessions (where laughter is emphasized).

The weekends are a major highlight in the lives of many on a path to spiritual growth.

The Creation Workshop

In mid-July, 1993, my friend Jeff encouraged me to participate in this three-part intensive workshop to create a cohesive team mentality that would move us forward on the road to wholeness and help us take charge of our lives.

It seemed like the 'California thing' to do. I didn't have much desire to do the California thing, but I was intrigued with the thought that the workshop might give me an additional edge on life— help me obtain a good job, or find 'Ms. Right'! It was an opportunity to shed more of my victim complex and blossom as a whole being. So although by this time I was tired of working through my 'stuff' I chose to attend the 'Creation' workshop.

One tool I learned about that weekend that stands out in my mind was called the 'Five Points of Power': pay attention; keep your agreements; speak the truth; be accountable; ask for what you want and take action! The group leader explained that these Points of Power are essential for building self-respect and formulating trust with others. I believe they are essential if you want to accomplish a goal in your life.

We sat in a circle challenging each other to shed our negativity toward others and ourselves, which started bringing old feelings of hurt to the surface. This was exactly the intention of the facilitator. He wanted to provoke an emotional reaction! As he encouraged us to release our deepest feelings, there came a sudden outburst from several of us. As the room thundered with the sound of music, our voices externalized the sounds of terror, grief and rage. Getting the feelings out of our nervous systems seemed to do us all good. The facilitator provided loving support as we let go of our accumulated stress. The result was an emotional shift to greater self-integration and self-realization.

We stood before out team members in our underclothes, primal selves revealing all. What could have been a degrading experience turned into one of profound beauty as we experienced being loved for just being ourselves.

I love myself just as I am!

The top of the telephone pole seemed a long way up. I climbed nearly to the top but couldn't seem to make the last step.

"You are loved by the Universal Spirit itself!" my partner shouted. "And I love you too!" Empowered by her expression of love, I pushed through the last of my resistance and reached the top of the pole.

Towering above the crowd below, my feet planted on the revolving disk at the top, I began to turn, my arms spread like an eagle. I became the eagle, soaring over the world. Revolving a full 360 degrees, I saw a trapeze hanging several feet from me.

The others shouted their encouragement from below. "Jump!" they cried. "Go for the trapeze! You can do it! The Universe loves and supports you!"

I shouted, braced myself, and jumped. My hands caught the bars of the trapeze. I had done it! What an empowered feeling! (I wore a safety harness as a precaution during this experience, by the way. I was brave, but not stupid).

One guy in the workshop (we called him 'Mr. Macho') couldn't seem to give up his disdain for gay men and women. The facilitator asked him to dance with me at a disco. While I am not gay, I had no prejudices against the gay life style or those who chose it; I'd worked with a variety of gay men and women and have gay acquaintances and friends.

"Sure," I said. "I enjoy dancing, and I guess I could dance with a man as well as with a woman."

Mr. Macho was very assertive on the dance floor. This was a tough assignment for him. I had a blast turning, twisting, rocking and rolling with him. I ended up on his shoulders, totally enjoying the moment as he groaned his disdain.

The facilitator asked me to determine my purpose in the world, and with his help I formulated it: 'to empower others to find themselves by sharing my loving insight.'

The workshop ended with a closing ceremony in which we passed a lit candle and each spoke our truth to the others.

After the ceremony music and laughter filled the room. We danced our heartfelt joy in celebration of life itself, releasing any remaining negativity. How sweet it felt to just let go! The dancing and the music were electrifying and magnificent.

Sadhana Fellowship Workshops

Over the weekend of January 24, 1998, I participated in a Rebirthing workshop at the Sadhana Fellowship. Tim facilitated as I stood there in front of the group with Jill kneeling in front of me playing the role of my mom.

I actually began to see her as my mom, and started to release my emotions. I was able to go to the core of my emotional anxiety, and I achieved a profound sense of release, the net result of which was greater self-confidence and awareness of others.

On February 11, a Wednesday evening, I attended a Spiritual Breath Work session. Here the facilitator aided me in my emotional release with Native American music that penetrated my defenses and helped me access my feelings. Through the circular breathing I began to connect with my sense of grief, and the tears started to flow. The breath took me into an altered state of being. Initially I found it a challenging experience, but soon I began feeling peaceful. When I moved into the emotional release state I began to differentiate between the trauma and myself. I became a being freeing itself from pain.

I had become a witness to my own trauma! This was an out-of-body experience. There was a definite 'looking in' sensation, a profound and crystal clear separation of self from trauma.

I released my feelings as wave after wave of emotion came to the surface. When the emotional release session came to an end I returned to a fully conscious state of being, totally aware and more present than before. I felt cleansed!

I was capable at that time and under those circumstances of experiencing a spiritual presence. I felt connected to a spiritual essence that encouraged me to continue feeling and expressing my feelings, so that my connection with 'God' became stronger. 'God' and I were one. The sensation was one of complete and total bliss.

There was also a sense of eternity, infiniteness, a knowing and yet not knowing. There was everything and there was nothing. I was floating at peace in time and space while remaining connected to Spirit in a loving, gentle and tranquil state.

I realized that opening my heart to the limitlessness of Spirit was a key to my sense of well being and connection to soul. I had to let go and surrender, allow Spirit to accept me into the world in a gentle, kind, patient, caring, and an affectionate way.

This was totally counter to my habit of being overly critical of myself. I allowed myself to receive love, light, and acceptance from Spirit. I opened my heart and allowed myself to receive! I was being kind and gentle *to me!*

The more I connected to Spirit, the easier it was to accept and be open to divine consciousness and abundance. My issue of emotional scarcity became insignificant.

This experience motivated me to apply what I had learned from accessing temporary freedom from pain to create a complete freedom from trauma and an ever unfolding sense of inner peace. I have succeeded in staying connected to Spirit by using the following affirmation:

'I am accepted into the World in a kind and loving way! I allow myself to receive'.

The weekend of May 2nd, 1998, I attended a unique workshop with Sadhana Workshop leader Cass Smith. The Rebirthing session began and I started moving back in time through the circular breathing, beyond my birth and into a past life!

The breath took me beyond the immediate present to a life in which I had experienced a horrible death. I relived that life! I begin to face and relieve the horrors of my death as a child during the holocaust, and more. I accessed, connected with, and released a sense of terror that had clouded my mind and sensations for ages!

That release brought me such a sense of security. Fear had melted away! Freedom had come!

Sensitivity Groups

Sensitivity Groups were very popular in the late 1960s and early 1970s. I participated in just such a group during my senior year at Bernard M. Baruch College in New York City. We sat in 'in-groups' and encountered each other in an attempt to create an awareness of our individual issues. At times this method was useful and other times it was just confusing because individuals were too emotionally defensive.

Points To Ponder

Workshops have helped me significantly in my journey toward self-realization. I have found that the dynamic interplay can create productive change and positive shifts in consciousness for those who are willing to do the work. Consider the following:

• Do you believe play can be a significant aid in self-realization? Could having fun make it easier to release emotional distress?

• What kinds of workshops do you feel you might find helpful on your path to spiritual development? How would you locate such workshops in your area?

• What is stopping you? What is it going to take to move you to take action?

Nineteen

Full Moon Over Angels Landing

Keeper of the heart, I call on you this day.
Whisper in my ear and comfort me.
Place your hand in mine and hold me tenderly.
I walk with you tonight faithfully.

And if I should fall and I am forced to crawl,
I will crawl straight through the night.
And when I stand, I will take your hand.
Together we hold the night.

Keeper of the heart, I call on you this day.
Whisper in my ear and comfort me.
Place your hand in mine and hold me tenderly.
I walk with you tonight faithfully

And when times are hard and an inch feels like a yard.
I will call you to help me through,
And I know you will come, like the day greets the sun.
When the morning is fresh and new

Keeper of the heart, I call on you this day
Whisper in my ear and comfort me.
And hold me tenderly
I walk with you tonight, faithfully,
I walk with you tonight, faithfully.

My experience has shown me that the more fun, play, and enjoyment I experience, the greater my expression of love and release of stress.

Angels Landing is a retreat hidden away in the hills of Julian, California. I made my way there one memorial weekend following a morning Religious Science service honoring the men and women who served in the U.S. Armed Forces.

There among the pines some fifty people gathered to have fun and celebrate life. For openers, we created beautifully decorative hats. Mine was multi-colored with flowers and ribbons, and feathers adorning the very top.

Karl Anthony and Jeanne, his wife of eight years, blessed us with their joy, laughter and song. Karl, a musician, travels around the world singing for universal peace. He is an annual visitor to the September Whole Being Weekend in Idyllwild, California, where he leads a Saturday evening celebration and the closing ceremonies. His music is playful, uplifting, inspiring, enlightening and festive.

Karl inaugurated the weekend with his spiritually rhythmic music, pulling us together as our voices melded in song. Our hearts warmed by the singing, we made our own facsimiles of angels from clay and displayed them for each other. Later that day we made improvisational forms from colorful spandex material and played with them in an open field, and took a walk in the woods to a hilltop viewpoint from which we observed the sunset.

It felt good to return to the retreat grounds and the warmth of a fireplace. We roasted marshmallows and participated in a sacred drumming ceremony, our version of a ritualistic experience found in indigenous cultures around the world, including many Native American cultures.

I'd always enjoyed experimenting with rhythm, and had participated in drumming experiences in a variety of workshops. I think drumming is fun, and I enjoy using it to connect with primal life force energy. One participant in this particular ceremony told me that the sounds of the drumming help a person to pass through and release emotional stress and connect with their soul.

That night Karl presented a concert in which he sang his beautiful 'Keeper of the Heart', the song featured at the beginning of this chapter.

Later that evening I stepped out into the chill air of the patio and observed a beautiful full moon over Angels Landing against a backdrop of clouds floating over and through the hilltops and mountains.

The next morning Karl's wife Jeanne treated us to a beautiful exercise session before breakfast. Several children read excerpts from a book reflecting the qualities of angels, and we ended the weekend with a talent show.

Points To Ponder

- Did you go camping with friends or groups you belonged to as a youngster? If so, what feelings does recalling that experience bring you now?
- How can gathering with friends to share song and fun enhance your experience of who you are as a human being?

Twenty

Devotional Singing

Devotional sings are spiritual in nature. Devotional musicians can inspire and uplift a group of singers to states of joyous consciousness. Devotional singing changed my life. I've been blessed to participate in a variety of contexts, including around the campfire at Whole Being Weekends.

My involvement with devotional singing began as part of a Sufi folk dancing retreat. Joining in a group sing gave me a sense of joyous enthusiasm. The words and melodies brought my attention into the presence as my distress and irritation gave way to peace of mind. The lyrics and melodies created an authentic heart opening for all present.

Devotional singing is found in many traditions, including Native American, Judeo-Christian, Islamic and African. The tradition here evolved out of the gatherings of young people during the hippie movement of the sixties and seventies.

Devotional singing merges spirituality with music. It is often performed in gatherings in private homes, with musicians playing guitar, organ, and drum. A guided meditation adds to the spirituality of the group sing.

Songs penned by Michael Stillwater reflect life transitions, such as birth and death. (A yoga practitioner, Michael has been inspired by the 'Course in Miracles'. He is also an artist and publisher of a humorous parody called 'A Course in Marigolds'). The songs of Robert Frey, John Astin and others touch on other themes. Following are some lyrics from some of their creations:

Lyric by John Astin:
Why have you come to earth? Do you remember?
Why have you taken birth? To love, serve, and remember.

Lyric by Robert Frey:

The light of Everyone's Love.
I am finding my divinity in the light of Everyone's Love.
Everyone's Love, Everyone's Love,
In the Light of Everyone's Love.

(The words HOLINESS, PERFECTION, and COMPASSION may be substituted for the word DIVINITY).

'Opening My Heart to Love' by Robert Frey:

I am opening to love,
I am opening to love,
I am opening to love.

Love is the feeling of living in my heart,
Love is the feeling of living in my heart,
Love is the feeling of living in my heart,
Of living in my heart.

I feel the love flowing through me.
Love flows through me now.

Lyrics by Michael Stillwater:

Be still and know you are God,
Be still and know you are God.

Lyric by an unknown author:

Keepers of the earth
Keepers of the wisdom,
Keepers of the love and the light.

Dance, Dance, Dance, Dance,
Wherever you are, Wherever you are.

Lyric by Nirava Seastar:

Take me in your arms, O mother!
Lead me to the other shore!
I let your love replace my fear.
I let my heart be an open door.

Heal me to the core, O mother!
Or

Illuminate my deepest truth, O mother!

Lyrics from the Jewish Renewal Movement (sung in Hebrew):
Let us invoke 'Hashem' (God), the Almighty God of Israel:
On my right stands Michael, on my left stands Gabriel;
In front of me, Uriel; Behind me, Rafael.
And above my head, the Shekinah, God's divine presence.

Points To Ponder

- Have you ever participated in a group sing? If so, how did it make you feel?
- Do you know of groups that get together in your area to sing for spiritual upliftment? If so, have you considered attending?

Twenty-one

Spiritual Touchstones
in Religious Contexts

Jewish Renewal Meditation Group

The Synagogues of San Diego have stirred my heart with services offering songs and prayers celebrating a belief in a Higher Power and thankfulness for the good in our lives.

The Jewish Renewal Movement has played a major role in my self-realization by bringing together Jewish concepts, honoring both prayer and meditation. The Jewish Renewal meditation group was established in San Diego by Rabbi Zalman Schachter-Shalomi. There are several meditation groups that meet within the heading of Jewish Renewal: The Elijah Minyan, Devotional Singing, and Chavurah (friends). These groups follow a joyful path of prayer, meditation, ritual, chant, song, and studying Torah.

Meditations are held at the home of a leader in the movement. Participants begin each meeting by standing in a circle, taking turns standing in the center surrounded by others who validate them with this prayer sung in unison:

May the Blessing of God Rest upon You.
May Gods Peace Abide in You.
Now and Forevermore.

The goal is to offer this prayer to the recipient from a heartfelt space in the hope that he or she will be able to receive it with an open heart! If and when heartfelt openness can take place, a loving spiritual experience is achieved.

We can choose to surrender our fear, anger and grief and allow ourselves to receive easily from others! It can take the effort of a breath, a conscious breath, breathed with the intention of releasing ourselves from the incarceration of our mind, body, spirit, and soul by inhibitions reflecting past and present hurts. The breathing releases us from our fear of loneliness and allows God's Peace to abide within, now and forevermore.

The leader at this particular session explained the significance of the Hebrew letters Aleph, Shin, and Mem, and introduced us to the mystic Jewish tradition known as the Kabbala. He explained how one's life of activity (Shin) needs to be empowered by unity (Aleph) and by harmony (Mem), and that this can be accomplished through meditation.

The group then began a five-minute meditation. My meditation produced two images: the symbolic Star of David and the Christian Cross. When I spoke about those images following the meditation, the facilitator responded that the Christian cross is symbolic of the Tree of Life, and that the Jewish Star of David is symbolic of the balance of Yin and Yang, unity of mother and father. He explained that the Jewish symbols for Spirit, or God (Yud, Heh, Vav, Heh) represent the male head, female shoulders, male torso and the female legs, the legs of the female being grounded in the symbol of the mother earth.

I felt a sense of harmony and unity as a result of this meditative process.

There are times when I use a powerful traditional chant of the Jewish people:

Shema Yisrael
Adonai Elohaynu
Adonai Ekhad

Listen, everybody,
The Source of All our Beings,
That Source is one.

Here is an example of another beautiful chant:

Elohai (2x) N'shama
Shenatata Bi T'hora Hi

The Soul That You Have Given Me, Oh G-d, Is Pure.

After our discussion we chanted a healing prayer, 'Elna Rfnan La', which means 'God, please heal'. We asked for healing of those we knew, of those unknowns to us, and of mother earth. Finally we chanted a very beautiful prayer that translates as 'From you I receive and together we share'.

Some of these prayers are used as songs in spiritual Sufi folk dancing as well.

The Church of Religious Science

The Church of Religious Science follows the principles of Ernest Holmes. A phrase from his book *Science of Mind* states: "The Mind of man is some part of the Mind of God; therefore it contains within itself unlimited possibility of expansion and self-expression."

This phrase carries what I perceive to be the basis for the activities offered by the Church of Religious Science. Those activities include men's and women's support groups, loving care groups, breath work groups, and *Course In Miracles* study groups. Morning and evening services led by Religious Science ministers and practitioners are particularly inspirational.

At church services there are usually trained counselors waiting in the rear of the main hall who are trained to counsel and offer prayers to help the parishioners with the concerns and challenges of life. The counselors at the church go through a rigorous three-year training program that includes classes in prayer treatment, meditation, self-mastery, background of Science of Mind, and practitioner training. They spend the final year in service to the church and the community, and are required to take exams and to make and pass an oral presentation of their expertise before a group of experienced practitioners prior to graduation. They are dedicated and committed individuals with a commendable ability to 'be there' in a consistent and empathetic way.

I have often found it comforting to receive spiritual counsel from a practitioner following a Sunday morning service. I asked a Religious Science practitioner to comment about her experience. The following paragraph is taken from the letter she mailed to me:

> *As a Religious Science practitioner, I am privileged to be and reveal the many faces of Spirit in my life and in others. Over the years, my experiences as a practitioner has been to move beyond the 'facts', 'appearances' or 'conditions' one may be experiencing and focus on the Spiritual Truth of the individual's wholeness, perfection and oneness with God. I am honored to be that Light, to be fully present as individuals transform into the True Self and allow Spirit to move in, as and through all areas of their life, as a conscious way of living."*

— Suzette Wehunt, RScP

Points To Ponder

- If you are a member of an organized religion, is it feeding you spiritually?
- How can you get more out of your religious affiliation?

Twenty-two

Other Workshop Experiences

Of Eagles, Angels and Doves

It was Easter in the rugged and beautiful Southern California mountains. Julian is apple country, and the delicious and sumptuous taste of the town's gold is never out of season.

Springtime was doing its best to chase winter away, but winter was stubborn, and a canopy of late snow covered the mountain trails, hills, canyons, valleys and secluded cottages. If you listened carefully, you could hear nature's spiritual voice echoing the patterns of the mountain winds, harp-like tones filtering through the branches of tall snowy pines.

Horses stood aimlessly in the corral, seemingly bewildered by spring's snowy arrival. Mules looked on equally confused by the restless reaction of the horses to this untimely snowfall. Geese and ducks squawked their impatience at the chill of this uncommon initiation of spring. The Billy goats gave little notice to their restless movements; perhaps their thoughts were more on filling their own bellies.

My friends and I always looked forward to the natural progression of the seasons, hoping for a renewal of our spirit and of the universal connection between communities. Desire for spiritual rebirth was almost palpable amongst the participants in The Course in Miracles workshop.

The crows, the self-proclaimed guardians of this mountain retreat, circled overhead or sat on telephone wires in a lazy, cavalier manner. Majestic observers of all that moved and held still, they appeared to be waiting for something to happen. We imagined them to be the psychologists of the surrounding hills.

I awoke that Sunday morning to a delicious breakfast of "sunrise over the nearby mountains." Water dripped from icicles suspended from snowy rooftops. I could see the footprints of small animals in the unspoiled fresh snow. Squirrels or birds, perhaps? I didn't know. I felt at peace in this pristine environment.

The fireplace was stocked with wood, and the strike of a match ignited its glowing energy to warm the main living room of the ranch house. The colorful flames moved in a wild rhythmic dance that constantly changed its direction. It was a perfect template for our own need to dance and connect to ourselves and to each other. We were here to create ourselves as more loving, anchored, and empowered people in our own world.

It was in this environment that thirty men and women, symbolically dressed in black clothing to reflect the dark sides of our personalities, participated in the 'Course in Miracles' Workshop.

We listened to readings on separation and unity, and heard of how the spiritual Leader Jesus had experienced the crucifixion, resurrection, and ascension. I reflected upon the similarities between the sequence of crucifixion, resurrection, and ascension and my experience of the access, connection, and release of feelings in my own Rebirthing practice. Perhaps Jesus in his forty days' journey in the desert had practiced a similar exercise to free himself from trauma? Could Jesus have connected with the Holy Spirit by way of Rebirthing and Healing Breath Work? Could Joshua, known as a man of breath and spirit, have learned the secret of connecting with the Holy One by way of an intuitive sense? Could Moses have descended from Mt. Sinai after a Rebirthing or Conscious Healing Breath session to deliver the Ten Commandments to the Israelites? This speculation plays constantly in my mind.

Robert Frey and Mary Brenda McQueen were the leaders of this 'Course in Miracles' Workshop. Robert sang his beautiful heartfelt song, 'Eagles and Angels', and the group took in the exquisite melody and loving words. Mary Brenda contributed her loving presence and gentle warm-hearted innocence. Some of the participants shared their poems and thoughts on personal growth and connection with Spirit.

On Sunday afternoon we changed our clothing from black to white, the color of renewal and enlightenment. As the weekend drew to a close we could not help but feel blessed by the birth of a dove-like presence within. 'Of Eagles, Angles, and Doves'.

Miracle Weekends

Miracle Weekends are held in Julian, California. These weekends bring together individuals from Religious Science and other churches to focus on The Course In Miracles and Sufi Dancing. The Course in Miracles offers enlightening principles that give meaning and direction to life.

The Needy Facilitator

I have found that occasionally a workshop turns out to be a workshop in reverse—that is to say, the participants end up doing their best to heal a tortured would-be leader. Such was the case with Harry.

Harry moved like a slow shadow through the retreat grounds. Short and stocky with a headful of curly brown hair, he had a boyish anxiety in his energy. Although his dark brown eyes seemed to radiate a spiritual presence, an intuitive sense of doubt and distrust made itself known to those workshop participants sensitive enough to connect with Harry's level of emotional disturbance. His passion seemed to bubble up from a deep, dark, impacted rage. Violent and unyielding, it screamed for attention. It was a boyish rage in an adult's body. The adult was asking in a gentle, unconscious way for kindness, attention, and—above all—acceptance.

The soul of this well-meaning but tormented man clearly yearned to be held in a warm, caring, tender way. His need for the love of a mother and father reverberated through the embraces he craved from the workshop participants. Reaching out hungrily for gentle sounds and caresses, he seemed unaware that the acceptance he sought could only come from within himself.

This man was eminently confused! His intentions were unclear. How could he lead a workshop for personal growth and unity, when he obviously needed to attend as a participant to explore and resolve his inner turmoil? The contradiction was disturbing.

The man had issues! We could see he was in need of a heartfelt healing from wounds inflicted in a tragic childhood, but would he allow us to help him with our love? Our best efforts met with the dogma and glib cover-up of a disconnected human being in irrational pain. He was inaccessible, obsessed with his need to find acceptance by filling others' needs. When we failed to go along with his dogma, he fell into invalidating outbursts. We couldn't support this, and spoke up in loving but firm tones against his denouncement of our fellow workshop participants.

His patterns of distress continued without resolution. Clearly, his healing would require a consistent effort on his part. We offered all the loving support we could and wished him well.

Not all workshop leaders are competent at what they do. Choose wisely. If at all possible, it is preferable to have some experience of the leader before you enroll in a workshop. Facilitators often offer free or low-cost introductory evenings that will give you an opportunity to determine the quality of their offering. Or, if you have friends who have attended a workshop you're considering, you can ask them about the person leading it. (Ask more than one person, if possible; we all have different tastes).

Points To Ponder

• Have you considered enrolling in a weekend workshop this season? Which one? Are you going to do it?
• Do you think you could learn anything of value from a needy workshop facilitator? Why or why not?

Twenty-three

Sufi (Spiritual) Folk Dancing: Dances of Universal Peace

The Sufi Prayer and Invocation of Hazrat Inayat Khan:

O Thou, who are the perfection of love, harmony and beauty, Lord of Heaven and Earth, open my heart that I may hear your voice, which constantly comes from within. Disclose to me your Divine Light which is hidden in my Soul, that I may know and understand life better. Most merciful and compassionate God, give me your great goodness, teach me your loving forgiveness, raise me above the distinctions and differences which separate me, send me the peace of your Divine Spirit, and unite me with your Perfect Being. Amen.

The Sufi Invocation:

Toward the one, the Perfection of Love, Harmony and Beauty, the Only Being, United with all the illuminated Souls, who form the Embodiment of the Master, the Spirit of Guidance.

With this invocation, the dancers for universal peace begin their soulful openhearted journey as one entity, celebrating life through spiritual dance.

Sufi Dancing is a unique spiritual experience. Hazrat Inayat Khan, a Sufi master, introduced it to the United States in 1910 from his native India. Ruth St. Denis brought together dance and spirituality in the 1920s, portraying divinity on stage. Murshid Samuel Lewis, influenced by both St. Denis and Hazrat Inayat Khan, brought us the Dances of Universal Peace in the 1960s, incorporating sacred phrases found in many religions. In the early 1980s a Center for the Dances of Universal Peace was established, which now officially lists four hundred dances, the sacred phrases associated with them, and spiritual traditions of the cultures from which they are derived.

Sufism, a spiritual tradition of surrounding the self with God and submerging it in love, places considerable emphasis on the evolutionary journey that connects human kind to each other.

A Sufi Dancing session, often two hours in length, includes a variety of songs honoring a variety of cultural traditions, including Islamic, Christian, Hindu, Hebrew, Sikh, Quaker, Buddhist, and Native American.

Sufi Dancing is a unique circle dance in which participants share a soulful connection with each other through loving gaze. Dancers move in a circle singing heart-connected poetic lyrics in orchestrated rhythm, usually to live music—guitar, drums, organ, and flute, for example. Facilitators help maintain a spiritual heart centered mood conducive to creating an inner environment of peace and harmony. Conscious use of breath facilitates connection with emotion and Spirit.

My first experience with Sufi Dancing was at Ananda Ashram in Monroe, New York, in the early '80s. The room was semi-lit. The facilitator reviewed the simple words and steps before each dance, and we began circling the floor hand in hand, singing and gesturing, touching each other in a sensitive, aware, non-sensual manner.

I experienced a spiritual awakening through movement and dance in a tender, loving, and caring way. I felt a genuine sense of peace, harmony, and above all, joy. It was remarkable how this mellow, loving, soulful session of Sufi Dancing had the power to transform my inner conflicts. Stress gave way to a sense of peace and harmony.

At times the dancers spun in celebration as we revolved around the circle. Spinning connected me with the unity of conception and Spirit as the music moved me into a meditative state. I connected to the spiritually significance of conception. I allowed myself to surrender to the music and the breath. Our diverse emotional and psychological defenses disintegrated and we became absorbed into spiritual oneness. I felt an anchoring of self and entered a blissful state of being.

It has been said that adding song to prayer is equivalent to praying twice. When you add movement to songful prayer, it is like praying three times. When you dance in a circle with a shared heartfelt energy, then it is like praying four times! Sufi Dancing accomplishes this goal.

Every dance ended with the sound of 'OM'. This sound has much significance as it reflects unity of self and connection to the whole of Spirit. The facilitator encouraged us to give each other a heartfelt hug at the end of the dance.

It is with some sadness that I write about Sufi Dancing, since two facilitators have passed away at a young age. I find their untimely passing unusual, but perhaps they were needed to perform their loving service elsewhere in the celestial universe.

Mark Siegchrist, a beloved leader of Sufi Dancing in San Diego County, passed away in 1998. Through his leadership and inspiration Sufi Dancing found its roots in the hearts of many devotees. He will be missed for his genuine kindness and unselfishness.

Points To Ponder

• Would gazing into another person's eyes for long periods of time, especially a person of the same sex, make you uncomfortable?

• Have you ever considered relating to the God and Goddess within other people, rather than to their human personalities? If so, what was your experience?

Twenty-four

The Sacred Ceremonial Sweat Lodge

Oh Great Spirit
Earth, Sun, Sky, And Sea
You are inside, and all around me

We are one with the light of the sun.
Oh, Oh, Oh, Oh, Oh.
We are one with the light of the sun.
Oh, Oh, Oh, Oh, Oh.

I became acquainted with the inipi, or sacred ceremonial sweat lodge, in the early 1980's at Ananda Ashram in the foothills of New York's Catskill Mountains. Since then, I have participated in a number of sacred ceremonial sweat lodges at Whole Being Weekends and other gatherings in California. Although inspired by Native American tradition, the sacred ceremonial sweat lodges I have attended have been adapted for non-Native participants. The following accounts of my experience at a ceremonial lodge in Poway, California:

I arrived late in the afternoon. There was a clear blue sky with warm friendly temperatures. A trailer, small tents, and the ceremonial sacred sweat lodge dotted the canyon's brown landscape. The ceremony began with an honoring of the six gates, or directions in a circular area known as the 'medicine wheel' symbolic of East, South, West and North. At the center stood the sweat lodge. Four of the 'gates' represented by bamboo poles surrounded the structure. The remaining gates represented Grandmother Earth with green designators of feminine energy and Grandfather Sky in blue. A seventh direction, that of Great Spirit, centered the altar in front of the sacred lodge.

Prior to entering the medicine wheel, we stood at the East Gate while the gatekeeper purified our bodies by smudging them from

head to toe with lit sage. The sage had been lit and blown out causing it to smoke. Purified, we were welcomed into the wheel by the
gatekeeper.

The lodge itself was constructed from willow saplings set in the
ground and bowed down to form a rounded top. Although traditionally animal hides were draped over the willow saplings, this lodge,
like many today was covered by blankets. At the center of the lodge,
a pit served as a reservoir of the red-hot stones. Fire Tenders spent a
great deal of time preparing red-hot stones just outside the sweat
lodge. The fire tenders would be bringing the red-hot stones to the
doorway of the *inipi* at the direction of the facilitator.

The altar in front of the lodge was adorned with items symbolic of
creation and spiritual purification. Owl feathers, a turtle shell, an animal skull, the body of a hummingbird, a basket of sacred herbs, a
bird nest, and the sacred pipe known to the Lakota Indians as the
chanupa graced the altar.

The facilitator sat cross-legged in the circle. Jeff Happy Bear Goss
was medium built, Caucasian American, with a sincerity of purpose
and many years of experience leading this process of spiritual and
personal growth. He assembled the participants and asked us to sit
in a circle in front of the lodge while he explained the significance of
ceremony. Traditionally, the circle provides symbolic virtue as well.

"The lodge represents the womb of the mother," he told us. "This
is a place where individuals can find a greater opening of their hearts
and grow in authenticity. "We come to the circle to give and to receive." "We come to the circle, and to the sacred sweat lodge, to grow
in our personal power." "We come to be ourselves and to speak from
our center." "This is a transforming process." "Be in your heart."

We shared our reasons for participating in the sacred ceremonial
sweat lodge. The reasons were as varied, as connecting with spirit, releasing stress from mind and body, honoring ancestors, and blessing
mother earth.

It was time for smoking the sacred pipe. The facilitator asked two
women to remove the pipe and its herbs from the altar and bring
them into the circle. It was explained that the stem of the pipe represented the male energy, while the bowl where the herbs were placed
represented the female. Saying a personal prayer, we each touched
the bowl and stem of the pipe to our heart. The pipe was then lit and

passed around the circle. Everyone had an opportunity to smoke from it. I felt the herbal power of the smoke as it entered my lungs.

Following this, we were given small rectangular pieces of colored cloth, one color for each of the directions. We said a prayer and placed tobacco into each piece of cloth then tied them into bundles on a length of string. We moved to the sacred sweat lodge in preparation for entering. Within the lodge, we hung our strings of prayer bundles above our heads.

Some sweat lodge traditions require nudity. Others require clothing when both men and women are attending. Ours was 'clothing optional'. Some group members wore swimsuits while others went bare skinned. We silently entered the lodge in a clockwise, east to west pattern, symbolic of the suns' path in the sky. We filled the lodges outer and inner rims around the center pit.

The facilitator explained four rounds of the evening. The first round encompassed gratitude and personal empowerment. The second round identified prayer for family, the earth, and others. The third round served as a release of anything not serving our highest good. The final round was visionary. Each member would silently open to enlightenment from Spirit. The rounds entailed placing seven nested stones within the central pit. The fire tender used a pitchfork to carry the stones to the *inipi.* With the antlers of a buck, the facilitator lifted the glowing stones from the pitchfork and placed them gently into the pit. This was performed in silence. I respected the commitment to detail from Jeff Happy Bear Goss, the facilitator.

Participants were permitted to leave the *inipi* during the first three rounds if they felt overcome by heat, and could only re-enter at the initiation of subsequent rounds. The lodge warmed until the heat grew extreme. We sprinkled herbs over the rocks, and their aromas intensified the purification process, helping to cleanse our bodies.

Individuals repeated prayers, songs, and chants, to divert our attention from the increasing heat. Enveloped in darkness, we sat next to each other. The ceiling rose perhaps twelve to eighteen inches above our heads. We were in our Mother's womb. The opportunity to purify ourselves intensified.

During the second round, I began accessing and connecting with my feelings by way of circular breathing. Using the circular breath methodology was a conscience decision on my part. There was the quick breath in filling my abdominal cavity with air and the slow exhale out. I felt terror—the terror of self-judgment! My teeth chattered. I was frozen. This astonished me. The lodge was quite warm. My chattering alternated with the sounds of gut-felt, primal utterances, relinquishing the ties to these core emotions. It felt euphoric. Others experienced similar emotional releases.

The heat in the *inipi* mounted, and access to my feelings seemed unending. The anxiety was unbearable. Nonetheless, I continued breathing to release my anxiety. I held a pillow over my mouth to muffle the screams and not disturb the others. I persevered with ceaseless tenacity. I allowed myself to surrender to the spiritual voice that was guiding me. I felt a loving, supportive hand reaching out, and I accepted. Inside the *inipi,* we became brothers and sisters, sharing the experiences of opening, and releasing ourselves. We became a community with heart-felt connection. We shared a spiritual presence.

Amidst the unbearable heat within the inipi, our support for each other made this a loving experience. I transformed.

My tenacity throughout the two-hour ceremony refused my departure from the darkness and searing temperatures within this sacred temple. Water was passed around several times, and I poured it over my head to relieve the unyielding heat. Some participants did leave, but the remaining members inside placed no judgements upon them. Fire tenders greeted them outside and with open arms.

Our final activity ended with singing of 'Oh Great Spirit'. Thereafter, we crawled from the lodge to the congratulatory embrace of the fire tenders. A cold shower invigorated our bodies. Forming a circle we shared our experiences. We spoke of the spirits within the sweat lodge, and of their contributions displacing our harmful energies. We offered a plate of food to Great Spirit. Having offered food to Great Spirit, we celebrated with a royal banquet of foods brought for the occasion.

Points To Ponder

- Do you think exploring the spiritual practices of indigenous peoples could add a dimension of richness to your life?
- What spiritual traditions would you enjoy exploring?

Twenty-five

The Tantra Experience

Tantra can be described as a weaving of the interconnectedness of all living things throughout the universe, said to extend beyond time and space. There are many types of Tantra. It is a tradition that comes to us from India and China. I can observe a Tantra experience by simply focusing upon a painting of the loving touch between mother and child. I am observing the weaving an interconnectedness of an embodiment of a loving energy between mother and child. The west has come to know Tantra as an opportunity for two individuals to express themselves with open hearts by embracing sexual and non-sexual intimacy on a spiritual level. Making use of the techniques of Tantra, partners can develop a supportive emotional, intellectual, physical, and spiritual loving connection with each other. To do so, they must be willing to risk being eminently vulnerable as they share their feelings and their energy with each other.

Tantra is also an ancient tradition for transmuting sexual energy into pure love. It promotes personal growth through authentic verbal communication, eye contact, and aware, sensitive touch. Creating an environment of ritual, togetherness, and communion, it encourages a deep level of trust that makes effective access to individual thoughts and feelings possible and opens doors to allow partners to acknowledge each other's truth, openly express their wants and desires, and get their needs met. As courage unfolds and prevails, the discipline creates a space within which it is safe to risk looking at old wounds and releasing emotional and physical pain. Supporting each other through breath, movement, sound, and intimate touch, partners can facilitate each other's healing in a loving way.

Tantra is an excellent vehicle for freeing up the dark emotional aspect of our personalities so that we can create more of ourselves, establish a positive anchor to our identity, and learn to share genuine love. I have found that its healing effects can be amplified by integrating Rebirthing, Healing Breath, and Primal Therapy into the practice. This combination can assist in releasing feelings and freeing up rigid behaviors to allow bliss and ecstasy to become more common in our experience.

Tantric ritual can play a significant role in opening individuals to experience their own authenticity. A Tantric couple maintains a special altar on which meaningful ritual items are displayed. These can include love charms, personal love symbols, drums, incense, aromas, photos (including childhood photos for connection with their inner child), music, feathers (for use in massage), chimes, bells, articles of clothing, and candles.

Partners learn to nurture each other by touching, bathing or massaging each other's bodies in an aware, fun, and sensitive manner, allowing the non-verbal power of sensation through touch to prevail. Loving touch and the reassurance of aware hugs and caresses add to the environment of trust.

Tantra uses the breath, sound, and movement to clear emotional blocks from the seven 'chakras', the major energy centers of the body. The chakras begin with the sexual center, the genitals, symbolizing survival, balance, grounding, and physical creation. The *Hara* center, the lower belly, symbolizes flow and equilibrium. The solar plexus, beneath the rib cage, symbolizes radiance and expansion. The heart center, at the midpoint of the chest, symbolizes love and compassion. The throat center, the voice, symbolizes communication and truth. The 'third eye' center, at the midpoint between the eyebrows, symbolizes creation. The crown center, at the top of the head, is our connection to Spirit, symbolizing transcendence. There are many tools available for clearing emotional blocks of fear, anger, and grief from the chakras. The Rebirthing Healing Breath, bioenergetic exercises, and Primal methodologies can be very helpful. Partners can create a love symbol (heart symbol or other special love shape) to use as a meditative object to mentally clear emotional blockages by way of the breath. They can take turns supporting each other in emotional clearing. Working together to clear blocks from the chakras enables the Tantric spiritual connection to flourish. It can free both partners up for sharing of energy through the energy pathways of the body, creating an experience of shared ecstasy that few Westerners even suspect is possible.

I've had a variety of Tantric experiences over the years, beginning in the early eighties. My first experience with Tantra was at an Ananda Ashram workshop in which we used our fingertips to explore and give sensitive and sensual affection. Touching with the fingertips is one of the most sensitive and caring ways to begin to embrace Spirit, for it is at the very tips of the fingers that sensitivity and electrical energy is at its most magical. The electrical energy that emanates from the fingertips heightens the connection and sensations between two people. I have learned that the energy from the fingertips can be increased by first doing a Rebirthing session, which can allow you to access and express the profoundest of feelings of love and set the stage for giving and receiving with an open heart.

The experience of a full body massage with fragrance and oils is another experience of splendor. (Choose a fragrance or oil that is the favorite of the person receiving the massage.)

It is wonderful to have a guided Tantra experience with sensual music being played in the background. Music makes it easier to relax and let someone else take the responsibility and initiative. I enjoyed one Tantra experience at a workshop presented by both male and female musicians; they shared in the playing of the music and in the directing of the participants' interactions. Giving and receiving loving touch as sensual Tantra music is being played is spiritually uplifting.

I experienced a playful Tantra experience with a partner through barefoot *sole*-ful communication. It was fun to relate to each other through the soles of our feet, and to connect to our life force and to Spirit in that way!

Tantra requires patience and practice from both individuals. This usually means partners should agree on a period of time, perhaps ninety minutes at a time, to experience a clearing and a sense of sharing and communion with each other. Tantra doesn't need to end in sexual intimacy, but if and when it does the spiritual experience can be exhilarating.

Heartfelt Relationships offer significant opportunities for focusing on and diagnosing our unique and problematic issues, for going deeper into the distresses that can bring about greater personal growth. The ability and willingness to confront the difficult issues revealed through heartfelt relationships cleanses us of all of that which seeks to hold us back from real love of self and others. Tantra offers us profound tools for opening to our beloved in ever deeper ways.

Points To Ponder

- What is your definition of intimacy? Does it include communion with Infinite Spirit?
- What might be the benefits of experiencing and sharing more playfulness and joy in your intimacy?
- Are you brave enough to try some new and different Tantric behaviors to find out whether they can create greater trust in your relationship?
- Are you ready to learn how to use your vital energy to help you to heal old emotional and physical wounds?
- Are you ready to expand the emotional and physical love between you and your significant other?
- Where in your community can you find a Tantra teacher?

Glossary of Terms

Acupuncture*: A form of health maintenance that stimulates the body's ability to correct and balance itself. Developed in China almost 6,000 years ago, it is based on the theory that the life force (*ki*, *qi* or *chi*) travels in a continuous flow throughout the body via a network of energy meridians. Disease is understood as the result of failing to maintain a balanced meridian system. The acupuncturist inserts hair-thin needles, usually disposable, at specific points along the meridians to correct the imbalance by stimulating or dispersing the flow of life force.

Ananda Ashram: The literal meaning of this phrase is 'blessed retreat'. I visited this retreat in Monroe, New York for a period of seven years and participated in a variety of spiritual programs there.

Angelnicity: The reappearance of symbolic angel figurines 'by coincidence'. There is a spiritual significance associated with the synchronous reappearance of angel figurines.

Bioenergetics:* A system of psychotherapeutic bodywork founded by Alexander Lowen, who was most directly influenced by the work of Wilhelm Reich. Bioenergetics is based on the interconnection between chronic psychological defense mechanisms, such as repressed emotional trauma, and rigid muscular tension. The tension, known as 'armoring', causes severe energy blockage in the body. Exercise,

---

*Based on definitions in *New York Naturally*, Community Resources for Natural Living.
**Based on definitions found in a copy of Taber's *Cyclopedic Medical Dictionary* #18

breathing, and psychotherapeutic emotional release techniques are used to release these physical and emotional blocks.

Breath Work:* In its simplest form, this term implies consciously directed breathing techniques for physical, mental or spiritual health. For example, calm methodical breathing is used for calming and relaxation, and forceful breathing for emotional release. Forms of breath work include Rebirthing, Holotropic Breathing, Essential Breathing, Middledorf, Vivation and Optimal Breathing.

Carpal Tunnel Syndrome:** Pain or numbness that affects some part of the median nerve distribution of the hand (the palm side of the thumb, the index finger, the radial half of the ring finger, and the radial half of the palm). It sometimes radiates into the arm.

Chi, Ki, Qi: These are the Chinese and Japanese words for the vital life force energy that exists in all living things. This is the energy that flows through the energy meridians of the body.

Circular Breathing: This type of breathing is used in the rebirthing process. There is a connected breath process. The goal is to access the feeling without any noticeable pause in the breath cycle. The goal is to have a relaxed exhale with little control. The breath is usually from the mouth.

Consciousness:** A state of awareness in which the individual is oriented to time, place, and person (i.e., is capable of knowing approximately the date, the nature of the environment, his or her name, and other pertinent personal data). Consciousness combines memories and the comprehension of external reality, as well as the person's emotional state and goals he/she wants to attain. It is, then, a significant part of what is described as 'personality' in the most all-inclusive sense.

Course in Miracles:* A set of three books that teach that forgiving others is the way to remember God and our oneness with creation. Thus the "Course" focuses on the healing of relationships. The Course originated in 1965, in response to a request from two psychologists for a better way of relating to others. Nominally Christian, A Course in Miracles deviates radically from traditional Christianity in that it deals with universal spiritual themes reflecting a wide variety of ancient texts. The Course integrates metaphysics with psychology and therefore can be called a "spiritual psychotherapy."

Dance of Universal Peace: The name given to dances that have spiritually empowering benefits.

Devotional Singing: Spiritual singing performed by groups of individuals with the goal of enhancing inner and worldwide peace.

Dyad: Developed by Barbara Fox White, this is an effective communication process for those in relationship. The goal of the Dyad is to create awareness (insights) that facilitate harmony.

Emotion:** A mental state or feeling such as fear, hate, love, anger, grief or joy arising as a subjective experience rather than as a conscious mental effort. These feelings constitute the drive that brings about the affective or mental adjustment necessary to satisfy instinctive needs. Physiological changes invariable accompany alteration in emotion, but such change may not be apparent to either the person experiencing the emotion or an observer.

Emotional Release: The release of feelings such as rage, grief, terror, with the goal of cleansing and healing the self as well as connecting with a spiritual entity.

Emphysema:** A chronic pulmonary disease marked by an abnormal increase in the size of air spaces distal to the terminal bronchiole with destructive changes in their walls. This can cause possible breathlessness during exertion.

Fear: An emotion that has impacted an individual in a definitive way caused by hurt, and trauma. Thus an unhealthy thought process develops and a false illusion is created that impacts reality. The hurt experience can result in a unconscious instantaneous thought process setting off emotional anxiety, caused by the painful past experience, and triggered by a similar present one. The individual once again experiences a threat to the self.

Feeling: This is an energy pattern of the body. Feelings can be defined as healthy or unhealthy and can lead to behaviors that are enhancing, or self-defeating.

Rebirthing Components: There are several components of rebirthing. They could include birth trauma, unhealthy or negative thoughts resulting from definitive experiences, someone having a death urge, and distress accumulated from past lifetimes. Leonard Orr made reference to these five components.

Frustration: We create frustration for ourselves (anger & sadness) when we maintain a thought in our minds and the thought cannot be manifested into reality.

Guru: A spiritual teacher.

Hazrat Inayat Khan: This man introduced Dances of Universal Peace, otherwise known as Sufi Dancing, to the Western World.

Hypertension:** A condition wherein the patient has a higher than normal blood pressure.

Inipi: The Lakota (Sioux) name for the Sacred Ceremonial Sweat Lodge.

Iyengar Yoga: A form of yoga that integrates alignment, balance, strength and flexibility of the body, mind, and soul. The literal meaning of 'yoga' is 'unification of the sun and the moon, union of the self'.

Jewish Renewal: A movement within the Jewish Faith that brings together Buddhist and kabalistic prayer, song, and traditional cultural activities to create a renewed spiritual awakening among the participants.

Kabbalah: A collection of teachings of mystical Judaism.

Kibbutz: An Israeli name given to a settlement of individuals who join together for the survival and betterment of the whole group.

Kinesiology Chiropractic: The study of muscles and body movement having the goal of making adjustments affecting the bones, joints, and vertebrae. A healthcare provider may place certain foods, vitamins, minerals, herbs, and homeopathic formulas under a person's tongue and test for muscle strength to determine appropriateness of the substance for the body.

Laughter: Humor is a wonderful expression of human joy where a person instantaneously connects with self. It is an immediate connection and release of energy, a part of self that is eternal and infinite.

Linear Time: The ability to use our intelligence, and our memory of the past in the immediate moment (hopefully free of past hurt and trauma) in order to create new visions of our future.

Loneliness: When individuals begin to think negatively about themselves because of not being together with another person. They may judge themselves harshly. Individuals create energy of sadness by way of their thoughts that could lead to depression.

Meditation: Focusing upon stilling the mind and coming into harmony with the soul. Mantras in the form of words or sound can be used to achieve the goal of harmony and peace. A human being can experience more clarity in thought and feeling by releasing compulsive thought through developing the power of observing the mind by meditating.

Migraine: These are terrible excruciating headaches with a variety of symptoms including: severe head pain (usually on one side of the head), blurred vision, sensitivity to light, and nausea. Migraine may result because of on going job stress or hormonal reasons.

Osteoarthritis:** A type of arthritis marked by progressive cartilage deterioration in synovial joints and vertebrae.

Perception- We use our five senses, intuition, past experiences (memory), alertness, awareness, situation, and circumstances to determine our reality in the present. Hurt and trauma creating illusions that impact reality can impact our perception and clarity.

Peer Co-Counseling: An approach wherein two or more individuals share a period of time during which they give and receive loving, aware attention to each other's upsets and feelings of distress. The two individuals are of equal status both employing a set structure. Counselors are trained to actively listen.

Positive Affirmations: The use of positive phrases to contradict negative thoughts brought about by hurtful experiences. An example 'I am good enough'.

Post-Partum Blues:** The 'let-down' feeling experienced for no apparent reason during the period following childbirth. The mother afflicted with this condition becomes tearful and irritable, loses her appetite, and finds sleeping difficult. The depression is thought to be due to hormonal changes as well as emotional needs arising during this period. Post-partum blues occurs in 70% to 80% of all mothers.

Power Breath: A breathing pattern used in the Rebirthing process wherein an individual takes nine quick inhales and exhales, then inhales and holds the breath, tightens all the muscles, and waits before exhaling. The goal is to release the deepest of emotions, allowing for profound cleansing and healing of self.

Primal (Scream) Therapy:* Based on the premise that trauma and unmet needs from early life create pain which are then often repressed, Primal Therapy allows an individual to relive and release imprinted hurtful memories through vocal expression of past trauma. Unacknowledged feelings and needs create neuroses by causing us to split off from our real selves as we try to obtain fulfillment in symbolic ways, which can include such physical and emotional symptoms as anxiety, migraines, asthma, heart disease and cancer.

Psychosis:** A term generally restricted to disturbances of such magnitude that there is personality disintegration and loss of contact with reality. The disturbances may be of psychogenic origin without clearly defined physical cause or structural change in the brain. Psychoses are usually characterized by delusions and hallucinations, and hospitalization is generally required.

Rebirthing:* A self-help method using a simple, defined circular breathing technique to achieve a finer awareness of mind, body and emotions and bring oneself fully into the present moment. In this state, the individual can experience an expanded awareness of previously submerged feelings and sensations. The significance of the use of the breath in this process lies in its profound connection to thoughts, feelings and memories. Rebirthing often allows us to re-experience the birth trauma, believed to be the source of the resistance, negativity, and feelings of rejection we carry into adult life. Rebirthing allows full surrender to self so that a natural, smooth restructuring may occur, leading to an overall sense of acceptance, renewal and gratitude for life. The Rebirthing process is best learned under the guidance of a trained professional Rebirther.

Reflexology:* A science and art based on the theory that the feet, hands and outer ears are 'maps' of the body, and that relaxing touch techniques for applying gentle nurturing pressure to specific 'pressure points' found on these extremities can have a positive effect on corresponding organs throughout the body.

As stress builds, the body begins to work less effectively, leading eventually to ill health. Repeated over time, this method of healing has often been reported to dramatically promote a wide range of health benefits ranging from relief of pain in the neck, shoulder and lower back to relief of allergic reaction, headaches, upset stomach and colon discomfort.

Reiki:* 'Universal life-force energy'. Reiki is a scientific method of activating and balancing the life-force energy (also known as *ki, qi, prana,* and *chi)* present in all living things. Light hand-placement techniques may be used on the body in order to channel energy to organs and glands and align the chakras (energy centers). There are Reiki techniques for lessening emotional and mental distress and chronic and acute physical problems, as well as for achieving spiritual focus and clarity.

This method of health maintenance and disease prevention can be applied to oneself or to others. Reiki can be a valuable addition to the work of chiropractors, massage therapists, nurses, and others for whom the use of light energy is essential or appropriate. It is an ancient hands-on healing modality originally developed by the Tibetans and rediscovered by the Japanese in the 19th century.

Religious Science, Church of: The spiritual sanctuary where the principles of Ernest Holmes' Science of Mind are practiced. This is a Church whose focus is spiritual growth and not of dogma!

Religious Science Practitioner: A trained counselor who listens to concerns and offers loving prayers in accordance with the principles of Science of Mind. Practitioners honor each person from a holistic viewpoint and acknowledge their basic loving nature.

Relationship Counseling: This includes a variety of counseling methods, such as mirroring, Re-Evaluation Co-Counseling, Dyad,

and Therapist Intervention. In all of these, the partners work together to create awareness of issues that impede harmony and well
being.

Sacred Ceremonial Sweat Lodge: A multifaceted ritualistic and spiritually evoking process based on (but not the same as) the lodge of
Native American tradition. The lodge represents the womb and is a
place for cleansing and healing of self, relationships, honoring spirit,
and mother earth. Physically, the lodge is a circular structure made
of willow branches, originally covered with hides but today usually
covered with blankets.

Sensitivity Groups: These groups were popular in the late 1960s
and early 1970s. Their purpose was to create an awareness of participants' issues through encounter and, if necessary, confrontation,
and to bring about constructive change in self-defeating behaviors.

Shiatsu: A form of Japanese massage using the pressure of the fingers (usually the thumbs) on the energy meridians of the body to improve health, vitality and stamina. Varying degrees of pressure are
used to balance the energy along the meridians.

Sufi Dancing: Circular dances that make use of movement and singing to enhance connection with Spirit.

Synagogue: A traditional house of spiritual worship for those of the
Jewish Faith.

Synchronicity: A term applied to a series of unrelated events that appear to be connected in time, working, moving or occurring together
at the same rate, unexplainable in a practical sense, but having a connected significance and meaning.

Tae Kwon Do: The Korean martial art of the hand and the foot used in
the protection, self-defense, and spiritual growth of the individual.

T'ai Chi Chih:* A Chinese Taoist martial art form of meditation in
movement, combining mental concentration, coordinated breathing,
and a series of slow, graceful body movements. T'ai Chi may be practiced for meditative and health purposes or, with increased speed,
the movements may be used for self-defense. The practitioner allows
the body weight to sink into the center of gravity (the abdomen) and
the feet; this relaxes and deepens the breathing, slows the heartbeat,

and improves digestion and various other muscular, neurological, glandular and organic functions.

Tantra: The weaving of energy and consciousness through transmutation of sexual energy. Tantra can be described as the weaving of the interconnectedness of all living things throughout the universe, said to extend beyond time and space. Tantra methods seek to develop an awareness and embodiment of this process.

Time Travel: Movement through states of consciousness whereby the individual accesses, connects with, and releases emotions using the circular breath.

Torah: The body of divine knowledge and law found in the Jewish scriptures and tradition.

Transcendence or **Transcendentalism:** A philosophy holding that ultimate reality is unknowable or asserting the primacy of the spiritual over the material and empirical.

Trauma:** An emotional or psychological shock that may produce disordered feelings or behavior.

Yeshiva: A school of religious study for those of the Jewish Faith.

Whole Being Weekends: The name of a series of seminars and workshops held every year in San Diego County, California. The YMCA of San Diego State University sponsors the weekend.

Bibliography

Aaron, David. *Endless Light: The Ancient Path of the Kabbalah to Love, Spiritual Growth, and Personal Power.* (Berkeley, California: Berkeley Publishing Group.) 1998.

Anand, Margo. *The Art of Sexual Magic.* (New York: G.P. Putnam's Sons.) 1995.

Beattie, Melody. *Codependent No More.* (New York: Harper Collins & Row.) 1987.

Bear, Sun. *Wind Wabun, and Mulligan, Crysalis. Dancing with the Wheel.* (New York: Simon & Schuster.) 1991.

Bradshaw, John. *Homecoming: Reclaiming and Championing Your Inner Child.* (New York: Bantam Doubleday Dell Publishing.) 1992.

Collins, Judy. *Singing Lessons. A Memoir of Love, Loss, Hope, and Healing.* (New York: Mitchell Ivers, Publisher.) 1998. (Devotional Singing.)

Dougans, Inge. *The Complete Illustrated Guide to Reflexology: Therapeutic Foot Massage for Health and Well-Being.* (Boston, MA: Element Publisher.) 1996.

Eden, Karan. (Yates, Keith). *The Complete Idiot's Guide to Tae Kwon Do.* (New York: Alpha Books.) 1998.

Eknath, Easwaran. *Meditation: A Simple Eight Point Program for Translating Spiritual Ideals into Daily Life.* (Tomales, California: Nilgiri Press.) 1991.

Fried, Robert. *Breath Connection.* (New York: Plenum Press.) 1990.

Gilman, Michael. *108 Insights into Tai Chi Chuan. A String of Pearls.* (Roslindale, MA: Ymaa Publishing.) 1998.

Grof, Stanislav. *Adventure of Self-Discovery.* (State University of New York: State University of New York Press, Albany, New York.) 1988.

Hay, Louise L. *You Can Heal Your Life.* (Carson, California: Hay House, Inc.) 1987.

Helms, Joseph M. *Acupuncture Energetics: A Clinical Approach for Physicians.* (Berkeley, California. Medical Acupuncture Publishing.) 1995.

Hendler, Sheldon Saul. *The Oxygen Breakthrough.* (New York: William Morrow) 1990.

Hendricks, Gay. *Conscious Breathing.* (A Bantam Book.) 1995.

Hendrix, Harville. *Getting the Love You Want.* (New York: Harper & Row Publishers.) 1998.

Holdway, Anne. *Kinesiology. Muscle Testing and Energy Balancing for Health And Well-Being* (The Health Essentials Series) (Boston, MA: Element Publishing.) 1997.

Holmes, Ernest. *The Science of Mind.* (New York: Dodd, Mead and Company.) 1938.

Jackins, Harvey. *The Human side of Human Beings. The Theory of Re-Evaluation Counseling.* (Seattle, Washington: Rational Island Publishers.) 1982. (Peer Co-Counseling.)

Janov, Arthur. *Primal Scream.* (Los Angeles, California. Newstar Media, Inc.) 1997.

Jarmey, Chris and Mojay, Gabriel. *Shiatsu. The Complete Guide.* (Hammersmith, London: Thorsons, An Imprint of Harper Collins Publishers.) 1991.

Klotz, Neil Douglas. *The Hidden Gospel.* (The Theosophical Publishing House.) 1999.
Leonard, Jim and Laut, Phil. *Rebirthing. The Science of Enjoying All of Your Life.* (Hollywood, CA: Trinity Publications.) 1983.

Mehta, Mira. (Collins, Elaine. Atkinson, Sue.) *How to Use Yoga: A Step-By-Step guide to the Iyengar Method of Yoga, for Relaxation, Health And Well-Being.* (Berkeley, California. Rodmell Press.) 1998.

Minett, Gunnel. *Breath & Spirit. Rebirthing as a Healing Technique.* (The Aquarian Press. An Imprint of Harper Collins Publishers.) 1994.

Miller, Carolyn Godschild. *Course in Miracles. Creating Miracles: Understanding the Experience of Divine Intervention.* (New York: H. J. Kramer Publishing.) 1995.

Muir, Charles and Caroline. *Tantra: The Art of Conscious Loving.* (Mercury House: San Francisco.) 1989.

Neihardt, John G. *Black Elk Speaks.* (University of Nebraska Press.) 1932.

Neihardt, Hilda. *Black Elk and Flaming Rainbow.* (University of Nebraska Press.) 1995.

Orr, Leonard. *The Story of Rebirthing.* (Pamphlet) December 1990.

Rama, Swami. Ballentine, Rudolph M.D. & Hymes, Alan M.D. *Science of Breathing.* (Himalayan Institute Press.) May 1998.

Rand, Willis L. *Reiki the Healing Touch.* (Southfield, MI: Vision Publications). 1998.

Ray, Sondra. *Celebration of Breath.* (Celestial Arts Paperback.) 1984.

Sams Jamie & Carson David. *Medicine Cards. The Discovery of Power Through the Ways of Animals.* (Bear & Company Santa Fe, New Mexico.) 1988.

Sky, Michael. *Breathing: Expanding Your Power & Energy.* (Bear & Company.) 1990.

Stillwater, Michael. The Celebration Songbook. (Santa Barbara, California.) Phone (805) 969-4550.

Thomas, Christina. Secrets. *A Practical Guide to Unlimited Possibilities.* (Chela publications). 1989.

Villoido, Alberto and Jendresen, Erik. *The Four Winds. A Shaman's Odyssey Into the Amazon.* (New York: Harper & Row, Publishers, Inc.) 1990.

White, Barbara F. *Dyad Book.* (Encinitas, California: Pacific Rim Press.) 1994. (Relationship Counseling Handbook.)

Wood, Douglas. *Old Turtle.* (Minnesota, Pfeifer-Hamilton.) 1992.

Contacts

Rebirthers & Healing Breath
Inspiration University
Leonard Orr
PO Box 5320
Chico, CA 96927

San Diego University of Integrated Studies
5703 Oberlin Drive
San Diego, CA 92121
1858-638-1999
E-mail Sduis@sduis.edu

Bobby Edelson
1749 Petra Drive
San Diego, CA 92104
1-619-232-2142

Cass & Shama Smith
PO Box 230604
Encinitas, CA 92024
1-760-753-9205

Kennedy Carr
Nirava Seastar
251 Village Run East
Encinitas, CA 92025
1-760-943-8269

Barbara Fox White
Bfoxwhite1@aol.com
1-760-943-1890

Angela Geary
3356 Second Avenue, Ste C
San Diego, CA 92108
1-619-549-0929

Dore Varmer
Minister-Certified
Sadhana Fellowship
1-760-943-1793

Joel Vorensky
Http://www.idaretoheal.com
info@idaretoheal.com
1-619-584-8093

Jim Dorenkott
E-mail Jimdorenkott@hotmail.com

Linda Inacay
E-mail Lindainacay@earthlink.net
619-640-5800

Bonnie Selva and Wendy Rudell
Optimum Health Institute of San Diego
6970 Central Avenue
Lemon Grove, CA
1-619-464-3346
http://www.optimumhealth.org

T'ai Chi Chih
Good Karma Publishing
PO Box 511
Fort Yates, North Dakota 58538
1-888-540-7459

TaeKwon-Do
Master Instructor
Mustapha Abdul'jalil
San Diego TaeKwon-Do
8898 Clairemont Mesa Blvd
San Diego, CA 92123
1-858-279-7779

Sacred Ceremonial Sweat Lodge
Jeff (HappyBear) Goss
1-760-736-6515
Iyengar Yoga
San Diego Yoga Studio
4134 Napier Street
San Diego, CA 92110
1-619-276-8766

Reiki
Mary Lee Reynolds
2555 Camino Del Rio South #201
San Diego, CA 92108
1-619-260-8211

United Church of Religious Science
3251 West Sixth Street
P.O. Box 75127
Los Angeles, CA 90020-5096
1-213-388-2181

Jewish Kabbalah
1-800-Kabbalah
http://www.Kabbalah.com

Reevaluation Co-counseling
Personal Counselors
719 2nd North
Seattle, WA 98109
1-206-284-0311

A Course in Miracles
Foundation for Inner Peace
P.O. Box 615
Tiburon, CA 94920-0615
E-Mail info@acim.org.

Dances of Universal Peace
PeaceWorks
Center for the Dances of Universal Peace, Inc.
444 NE Ravenna Blvd, Suite 202
Seattle, WA 98115-6467 USA

Workshop Leaders
Karl Anthony
PO Box 130296
Carlsbad, CA 92013
1-760-434-5554
1-800-843-0165

Scott Kalechstein
http://www.scottsongs.com
1-760-753-2359

Robert Frey
E-Mail at rafrey2@aol.com

Acupuncture
http://www.acupuncture.com

Tantra
Http://www.tantra.com

About The Author

Joel Vorensky embodies the understanding that wisdom comes through doing.

His first 'doing' was a childhood job shoveling snow. Since then he has worked as a typist; as a taxicab driver in New York City and San Diego, California; as a stevedore (longshoreman) on the docks of Copenhagen, Denmark; as a teacher of both adults and children in private and public schools in the U.S. and abroad; and as a retail salesman, registered securities representative, bank officer, insurance broker, bookkeeper, baker, agricultural laborer, crowd control officer, ice cream parlor cashier, hospital clerk, liquor store clerk, mailroom clerk, and restaurant busboy.

Teaching and counseling has been a consistent theme in his life: languages (English As A Second Language, Swedish, Spanish, Hebrew, Latin, and Greek) as well as medical terminology, computer software, business insurance and marketing. He has taught at the American Language Institute at San Diego State University, in public and private adult and elementary schools, and in adult detention centers. Mr. Vorensky has a 28-year background in peer counseling in the English and Scandinavian languages.

The work he has found most enjoyable and rewarding has been within the helping professions: as a peer counselor, hospital orderly, community liaison worker for immunization, public health advisor for communicable diseases, hospital admitting representative, support person in credit and collections at a children's hospital, and medical secretary for a neonatology intensive care unit.

Joel grew up in Queens, Brooklyn and New York City. He lived in Scandinavia for seven years and spent several years in the Middle

East. For the past fourteen years he has made his home in San Diego, California, the city that has served as a springboard for his extensive travels. He has a daughter, now grown, currently studying in Honduras.

Since 1968 he has been on a conscious path to heal the pain that began in the trauma of his birth, a path that has taken him on an odyssey through the various personal growth and healing modalities available in the Western world.

Joel holds a degree in business and a Scandinavian teaching certificate in early childhood.

The eclectic nature of his experience has afforded him social exposure leading to significant insights as to 'what makes people tick'. In this book he freely shares his wisdom with all who care to listen and apply it to the task of improving their own lives.

Order Form

Please send me ___ copies of
I Dare To Heal: With Compassionate Love at $14.95 each.

Book order: $_____

7.50% sales tax (California orders only): _____

Shipping: _____

U.S. Orders: $4.00 for first book, $2.00 for each additional book
International: $9.00 for first book, $5.00 for each additional book

Total: _____

❑ My check/money order for $_____ is enclosed
Please charge my ❑ visa ❑ MasterCard ❑ Discover card

Account Number _____

Expiration date _____

Name on Card _____

Daytime phone _____

Name on Card _____

Signature _____

Send to:

Name _____

Address _____

_____

City, State, zip _____

Life's Breath Publications
6394 Rancho Mission Rd. Suite #116
San Diego, CA 92108
www.IDareToHeal.com
Info@IDareToHeal.com
619-584-8093/619-640-0573 (fax)
Credit card orders: 866-292-8022 (toll free)
Satisfaction Guaranteed!

Order Form

Please send me ___ copies of
I Dare To Heal: With Compassionate Love at $14.95 each.

Book order: $_____

7.50% sales tax (California orders only): _____

Shipping: _____

U.S. Orders: $4.00 for first book, $2.00 for each additional book
International: $9.00 for first book, $5.00 for each additional book

Total: _____

❏ My check/money order for $_____ is enclosed
Please charge my ❏ visa ❏ MasterCard ❏ Discover card

Account Number _____

Expiration date _____

Name on Card _____

Daytime phone _____

Name on Card _____

Signature _____

Send to:

Name _____

Address _____

_____

City, State, zip _____

Life's Breath Publications
6394 Rancho Mission Rd. Suite #116
San Diego, CA 92108
www.IDareToHeal.com
info@IDareToHeal.com
619-584-8093/619-640-0573 (fax)
Credit card orders: 866-292-8022 (toll free)
Satisfaction Guaranteed!